THE PSALMS IN THE JEWISH CHURCH

THE PSALMS IN THE JEWISH CHURCH

BY THE REV.

W. O. E. OESTERLEY, D.D.

(Examiner in Hebrew and Greek Testament in the University of London)

AUTHOR OF "OUR BIBLE TEXT," "THE JEWISH DOCTRINE OF MEDIATION," ETC.

Wipf & Stock

PUBLISHERS

Eugene, Oregon

Wipf and Stock Publishers
199 W 8th Ave, Suite 3
Eugene, OR 97401

The Psalms in the Jewish Church
By Oesterley, W. O. E.
ISBN: 1-59244-698-1
Publication date 5/10/2005
Previously published by Skeffington & Son, 1910

PREFATORY NOTE.

An apology is perhaps needed for writing a book on the *Psalms*, a subject which has been so admirably treated by a number of the most eminent scholars, which has been approached from almost every conceivable standpoint, and which, therefore, embraces a literature which is already exceedingly voluminous. The writer's apology must be that, in spite of all that has been written, there is one aspect of the subject which, he ventures to think, has not been sufficiently taken into consideration, namely the *Jewish*. The attempt is, therefore, made in the following pages to give some idea of the place which the Psalms have occupied, and do now occupy, in the Jewish Church. This, it is true, involves touching upon some subjects which have been far better treated by other writers; but in dealing with the place and use of the Psalms among the Jews, such topics as their musical accompaniment, their poetical structure, etc., can scarcely be left out of account. The author has, however, sought to lay more stress on matters which are, as a rule, not dealt with, or only incidentally touched upon, in Commentaries on the Psalms, and the like. Excepting in the case of the introductory chapter and the final one, use has been made, in the main, of Jewish authorities, a fact which, it is hoped, may make the book useful to some who have not access to this class of literature; thus, the information to be gained from Mishnic tractates and from Midrashic works has been freely utilised, while the works of modern Jewish scholars, both German and English, have afforded the writer a great deal of help.

For one who is not a Jew either by race or religion to take upon himself the task of discussing the Jewish use of the Psalms may appear presumptuous; but the sympathy engendered by personal intercourse with Jews, interest in Jewish institutions, and the study of Jewish literature, can to some extent qualify a Christian to write on things Jewish, even though in many respects he may feel the want of more adequate knowledge.

The writer desires to express his hearty thanks to the Rev. G. E. Friedlander, minister of the Western Synagogue, for a number of details which were of much help in writing Chapter IX., "The Psalms in the Modern Synagogue"; also to Miss Dampier for supplying him *data* regarding the use of the Psalms in the Sephardic Ritual. Thanks are also due to the Rev. Sir W. Robertson Nicoll for permitting the writer to reprint his "Commentary on Psalm xci." from the *Expositor*.

W. O. E. OESTERLEY.

Hatch End, Middlesex,
October, 1910.

CONTENTS.

Contents.

CHAPTER III.

CHAPTER IV.

CHAPTER V.

Contents.

Contents.

CHAPTER IX.

CHAPTER X.

CHAPTER XI.

CHAPTER XII.

THE PSALMS IN THE JEWISH CHURCH

CHAPTER I.

INTRODUCTORY.

SOME DATA FOR DETERMINING THE CHARACTER OF MUSIC AMONG THE ANCIENT HEBREWS.

It is often said that we are wholly in the dark regarding the musical performances, whether vocal or instrumental, of the Hebrews; in a modified sense it is, perhaps, true to say that "we know nothing whatever of the nature of the music performed by these (Hebrew) singers and players";[1] nevertheless, there are certain lines of investigation which, if carefully followed out, will, we venture to think, be not without results in enabling us to form some definite ideas as to the character of both vocal and instrumental music among the ancient Hebrews. It is proposed, in the present introductory chapter, to indicate briefly what these lines of investigation

[1] J. Millar in Hasting's *Dict. of the Bible*, iii. 547.

are; not to follow them out in detail, but merely to show, by a few examples, that a more adequate study of them would, in all probability, yield really tangible results. But even the cursory glance which it is here intended to give may, it is hoped, be to some extent helpful in obtaining some idea of the music among the Hebrews as it existed both in the very early days of their history, as well as in later times, after the Exile and onwards, when music played such an important part in the Temple worship.

We shall, therefore, first of all, make a brief reference to some of the *data* regarding the earliest forms of music known to us. There are certain fundamental facts concerning music, which seem to be in accordance with natural laws, and may therefore, presumably, apply to the ancient Hebrews as they do to the men of every other race whose music has been studied. In the next place, a few details of ancient Egyptian music will be considered, together with a glance at its form among modern Egyptians, for evidence is forthcoming that in some respects the latter has close affinities with the former. The well-known conservatism of Oriental peoples is a factor not to be lost sight of in this connexion. Egyptian influence upon the Hebrews has during certain periods of their history been very marked, and it is more than probable that this influence was exerted in the domain of culture as well as in other directions. Music among the Assyrians will also be referred to, for they, too, exercised a great influence over the Hebrews, during the seventh and eighth pre-Christian centuries. In later times Hellenic culture left indelible marks upon the Hebrews, and the supposition is reasonable that here, too, musical taste was affected ; so that some reference to music among the Greeks must also find a place. Lastly, and perhaps most important of all for gaining some idea of Hebrew music in ancient times, there is the music of the Arabs ; a few words will, therefore, also be said about this.

§ I. *The origin of "Music."*

The desire to express the emotions is proper to the whole of animated Creation ; and the chief, though not the only, way whereby the inward working of emotions is made outwardly apparent is by means of vocal expression. But the existence of variety of emotion demands a corresponding variety in the mode of expression; this is true of the lower Creation, as well as of man; for example, the difference between the joyous bark of a dog, a growl of anger, and a whine expressive of pain—some of Nature's primitive "musical" sounds—is recognised by dogs themselves; and it is at least conceivable that something corresponding to these audible expressions of joy, anger, pain, etc., exists in a considerable portion of the Animal Kingdom, even though man may be unable to detect them in some cases. The most beautiful of Nature's music is, of course, the song of the birds;

it is, therefore, to be expected that among some specialists it should be held that music first came into existence among men from the desire to imitate the song of birds. As far as is known, Lucretius[1] was the first to put forth the theory that men first learned music from the birds.

"Other theorists," according to Dr. C. S. Myers,[2] "looking to the value of rhythmical music in furthering work[3] and dancing, and having regard to the delight taken by primitive people in the beats of the tom-tom, have laid chief stress on rhythm as the source of all music." This theory fails, apart from other reasons, in view of the fact that examples of primitive music exist which "are characterized by a total absence of rhythm."[4] More plausible is the suggestion, also mentioned by Dr. Myers, which has been put forward that "music began when primitive man vied one with another in exhibiting his superior attractiveness before women";[5] this theory is presumably based upon the analogy of a similar procedure in the lower creation,[6] and it only takes one type of emotion into consideration, whereas those of joy, sorrow, and anger, are just as elemental in human nature as the erotic emotion. Theorizing on

[1] In his *De rerum natura;* quoted by Forkel, *Allgemeine Litteratur der Musik*, p. 3 (1792); Lucretius lived in the former half of the first cen. B.C.

[2] "The Ethnological Study of Music," in *Anthropological Essays* (p. 237), 1907.

[3] For examples of this, see p. 16. [4] *Op. cit.* p. 237. [5] *Ibid.*

[6] See the section on "Sexual Selection" in Darwin's *Origin of Species*.

the subject is exceedingly fascinating, but it is also very precarious, for in our present state of knowledge, we are largely working in the dark ; far more numerous and reliable *data* are required than are at present available before our knowledge of the place of music among uncultured peoples, their ideas of rhythm, melody, harmony, tonality, pitch, and intervals, is sufficiently increased to enable us to arrive at scientific conclusions based on the sure ground of ascertained facts. Some *data* we have ; these will be referred to presently, and as far as they go they are of value, but they do not go very far. At present it is safest to say, concerning the origin of music, with Dr. Myers that "we may regard musical and verbal language as derived from a common source; namely, from the tendency to give vent to feelings by vocal expression."[1]

§ II. *Music among uncultured peoples.*

Uncivilized man is stirred most by the rhythmical element in music ; "the widespread occurrence of complex rhythms among primitive peoples is perhaps intimately related to their generally scant feeling for harmony." [2] The emphasis laid on rhythm, which has been noticed among savages all the world over, is a fact of the highest importance, we shall have to refer to it again more than once. The immediate result of this characteristic in very early forms of music is that it, almost of necessity, excludes the use of any great

[1] Myers, *Op. cit.* p. 237. [2] Myers, *Op. cit.* p. 237.

compass; the number of different notes used must necessarily be small; and this is exactly what is found to be the case in the most primitive forms of music known. Another result which follows naturally is that no great importance is attached to melody; if rhythm is more important than melody, it does not matter much, it would seem, what the melody is, and one can well understand that one melody should do duty on all sorts of occasions, which, again, is actually the case among primitive peoples. In speaking of music among savage races Ambros[1] says, that if there is a melody among them it is of the most primitive kind, and it is brought forth originally on the spur of the moment; if it finds favour it is repeated again on all kinds of occasions; in this way, he maintains, folk-song first originates. The following example is given; it was obtained by the Polar explorer, Elisha Kent-Kane, from the Eskimos of Anoatok:—

With strongly marked rhythm this is repeated over and over again. Here is another example from the same source, which well illustrates the characteristic of constant repetition:—

[1] A. W. Ambros, *Geschichte der Musik* (1887), Second Division, *Die Musik der Culturvölker des Orients*, pp. 538 ff.

It is interesting to notice in this example how the rhythm comes to the fore; if one hums it one will inevitably accentuate the second *c* in each bar. Both examples illustrate very pointedly some words of Dr. Myers; in discussing the subject of tonality among primitive peoples, he says: "By the feeling for tonality we mean the underlying recognition of a tonic; that is to say, a certain tone of a melody is regarded as the centre of gravity, to which all the other tones come to have a felt reference, and seek, for the sake of restfulness, to return. The tonic is not necessarily the lowest, nor need it be the final note of the melody. The feeling for tonality may have developed *pari passu* with the growing feeling for harmony; but in a low degree it may certainly exist independently of the latter."[1] The second of the above examples illustrates also another fact, and that is that the earliest intervals, apart from the octave, which were apprehended, were the *fifth* and the *fourth*. This apprehension of the perfect intervals before the imperfect seems to be in accordance with a natural law; the distinction between the two has been observed for many centuries, says Mr. R. H. M. Bosanquet, "but neither ancients nor moderns have adduced any explanation of the phenomenon, and the

[1] *Op. cit.* p. 246.

wondrous fact that perfect intervals differ in constitution and treatment from other intervals appears to defy reason, and not even to incite speculation."[1] The following Soudanese melody, which is repeated many times, again illustrates what has been said[2]:—

The natives of the Sandwich Isles, we are told, know only four notes, together with the octave of the lowest of these ; so, too, the natives of Tongatabu, who also know only four or five notes, but not the octave of any of them ;[3] of an even less developed type is the music of the natives of Tahiti, which is a "sleep-inducing murmuring without a vestige of melody or any kind of time."[4] How similar in general characteristics the music is of uncultured peoples in widely separated parts of the world will be seen by comparing the following examples with those already given. Two Jesuit missionaries working in Abyssinia took down from the natives there these two very simple melodies[5]:—

[1] *Encycl. Brit.* xvii. 78 (ninth ed.). [2] Ambros, *Op. cit.* p. 546.
[3] Ambros, *Op. cit.* p. 543. [4] *Ibid,*
[5] J. N. Forkel, *Allgemeine Geschichte der Musik,* i. 94 (1788).

Quite similar melodies are to be heard among the North American Indians.[1]

The next is a melody sung by the Maoris of New Zealand [2]:—

An interesting thing about this melody is that while it was being sung some of the natives joined in, singing it a third lower; that points to a great development in musical culture among the Maoris, which is further illustrated by the following dirge, sung very slowly [3]:—

One other example may be given here; it is of special interest, for it offers a fully developed theme, while its rhythmical character is strongly marked; it is from Senegal [4]:—

[1] Ambros, *Op. cit.* p. 541. [2] Ambros, *Op. cit.* p. 545.
[3] *Ibid.* [4] Ambros *Op. cit* p. 546.

Though somewhat monotonous when repeated many times, this would make quite a passable march; its developed character is certainly striking, and it would be both interesting and important to know whether it belongs to the older music of the Senegalese or not; for, as Dr. Myers says, "some of the changes which the music of a given people has undergone in the course of its development may be revealed by a careful comparison of the older with the more modern tunes." And he goes on to say, what is as true as important, that "nearly every people, however primitive, preserves what we may term its classical music. Such music often becomes invested with a sacred character. It may be performed only in secret initiation ceremonies, or during religious observances. In this connexion the native myths regarding the origins of music and musical composition should be studied."[1]

It should be mentioned in connexion with the examples of melody among uncultured races given above, that in almost every case they are accompanied by a dance, and it is the dance which gives the rhythm to the music.[2] Ambros, from whose important work most of the examples are taken, lays special stress on this fact; this only further emphasizes the truth that among primitive folk rhythmical accentuation is more

[1] *Op. cit.* p. 240.

[2] For examples of the combination of dances and singing, usually in ceremonies of a religious character, see J. G. Frazer, *The Golden Bough*, i. 33 ff., 465; ii. 326 f., 381 ff.; iii. 255, etc., etc. (1900).

easily perceived than variations in tone; the organ of time manifests itself more than apprehension of tone distances. It follows, therefore, that what one may call the "recitative" mode preceded melody in the stricter sense. Finally, in the words of Dr. Myers: "In the tunes of very primitive people, who always sing in unison, and have no knowledge of polyphonic music, we often meet with successive tones which, if sounded together, would pronounce true consonances. It has been suggested that such consonances have been actually heard by these people, owing perhaps to their chance occurrence in nature, or to the occasional want of strict time when members of a chorus are singing together. We may reasonably question whether such accidentally occurring instances of fusion are responsible for the existence of harmonic intervals in the melodies of very primitive folk who never practise polyphonic music. The appreciation of a relation between consecutive tones is a far more plausible explanation, but we are entirely ignorant of the psychological and physiological basis of such appreciation. So far as the smaller intervals are concerned, we have to bear in mind that approximately whole-tone and semi-tone intervals (seconds) are exceedingly common among such people, and that in folk-music generally the frequency with which the various intervals are used decreases proportionately with their size. It is highly probable that the smaller intervals have been determined rather by the feeling for equal tone-distances than by the feeling for simultaneous harmony. The feeling for tonality may also have helped in the definition of and preference for the smaller intervals in melody."[1]

It will be well to summarize now the main points yielded by our cursory survey of music among uncultured races.

i. The *origin of music* is wrapped in obscurity; but it can be said that it is due to the desire, universal in Creation, to express the emotions; this is done primarily and mainly by vocal expression. There is variety in this mode of expression because there is variety in the emotions to be expressed.

ii. Among uncultured peoples the *rhythmical element* is of far greater importance than the melodic; this characteristic asserts itself also in more developed forms of music.

iii. The *number of tones* known to men of limited culture is restricted to four, or five at the most.

iv. The earliest *intervals* apprehended are the perfect intervals, *i.e.* the octave, the fifth, and the fourth; this is probably the order in which they became apprehended.

v. Primitive *melody* is of the simplest kind; it probably did not consist of more than the equivalent of two bars originally, which were repeated many times, on different occasions; and therefore, presumably different sets of words were sung to the same melody.

[1] *Op. cit.* p. 246.

vi. The feeling for *tonality*, *i.e.* the underlying recognition of a tonic, is seen to be a characteristic of the melodies of uncultured races.

vii. The most ancient among the melodies of primitive peoples tend to assume a *sacred character;* this fact justifies the belief that many of the folk-songs among such peoples are of great antiquity.

viii. Among uncultured races there is an indissoluble connexion between *dancing* and music ; the former gives the rhythm to the latter.

ix. The "*recitative*" *method* preceded melody in the stricter sense ; this was necessarily the case, owing to the fact that the rhythmical element was more important than the melodic.

x. *Polyphonic music* is unknown among primitive folk.

These points will be seen to have a not unimportant bearing on the subject of music among the ancient Hebrews ; for they hold good regarding the music of races in widely separated parts of the world, a fact which suggests that they represent some fundamental elements in music which are common to all races of men.

For further details regarding music among uncultivated peoples, see Ambros, *Op. cit.* i. pp. 537-548 ; J. G. A. Forster, *Reise um die Welt während der Jahren*, 1772-1775, i. 166, 221, 343 ; ii. 252 ff., etc., etc.

§ III. *Music among the ancient Egyptians.*

According to Plato,[1] the Egyptians said that their

[1] Born 428 B.C.

most holy melodies originated from Isis,[1]; this suggests great antiquity regarding these melodies, which agrees with the well-known conservatism of the ancient Egyptians, and illustrates what was said above regarding the antiquity of sacred songs among uncultured races. An extremely interesting piece of information is given us by Herodotus,[2] who, in speaking of music among the Egyptians, says: "They have, among other strange pieces, a song which is sung in Phœnicia, Cyprus, and elsewhere, but which goes by a different name in each race. It is similar[3] to that which the Greeks sing under the name of *Linos.* I marvel concerning many things in Egypt, and I also wonder how ever it was that they got hold of the Song of Linos; yet, as it seems to me, they have been accustomed to use it from time immemorial. Linos is called Maneros in the Egyptian language, and was, as they tell, the only son of the first King of Egypt,[4] and his early death was mourned in dirges. This is said to be their first and only[5] song.[6]" Herodotus is here referring to a legend which, in different forms but with the identical underlying idea, was very widespread among the nations of antiquity; for this Linos-dirge[7] is the same as the

[1] *Cp.* Ambros, *Die Musik der Culturvölker des Orients*, p. 347.

[2] Born 484 B.C. [3] συμφέρεται.

[4] *I.e.* Menes, not a god, according to Wiedemann.

[5] This is obviously a mistake.

[6] ii. 79; Wiedemann, *Herodot's Zweites Buch*, pp. 333 ff. (1890).

[7] It is a confusion of ideas when Plutarch says (*On Music*, § iv.): "At the same time [*i.e.* when Amphion discovered how to accompany song

"mourning" for Adonis, Tammuz, Attis, Osiris, Lisyerses,[1] which was known and sung in Syria and Babylonia and Phrygia, as well as in Egypt and Greece. That the Israelites observed this annual mourning is clear from Isaiah xvii. 10, 11, Ezekiel viii. 14, Zechariah xii. 10, *cp.* Judges xi. 40. The legend which attached to the name of Adonis[2] was only a later "explanation" of the original celebration of the rite; Adonis was "one of those local gods who live with and in nature, who suffer in summer's drought, die with the winter, and live again with the early spring;"[3] hence the rite was twofold, the mourning for the death of the god, and, afterwards, rejoicing for his resurrection. The "strange pieces" to which Herodotus refers in the quotation given above were evidently popular folk-songs; the words of one such song has come down to us, for on one of the Egyptian monuments are depicted representations of oxen treading out corn (*cp.* Deut. xxv. 14), with the following inscription:

"Thresh, ye oxen,
Thresh the sheaves;
Thresh for your owner,
Thresh for yourselves."

with the *Kithara*] he [*i.e.* Heraclides] says that Linos of Eubœa . . . composed dirges" (ed. Westphal, p. 3). Linos, or Linus, is a shortened form for Ailinus, and is in reality only the cry *ai lanu* ("Woe to us") which the Phœnicians uttered when they mourned for *Adon* or Adonis.

[1] *Cp.* J. G. Frazer, *Op. cit.* ii. 224 f.

[2] See Lucian, *De dea Syria*, § vi. ff.

Encycl. Bibl. i. 69.

[4] Ambros, *Op. cit.* p. 348.

Similar songs, which are sung during labour, whether while harvesting, or at vintage-time, or while rowing, drawing water, etc., are habitually sung in Eastern countries even at the present day; they consist of very few notes which are sung over and over again, and the rhythm is set by the particular work engaged in at the time. The monuments of ancient Egypt, which have preserved for us *data* regarding both private and public life, teach us that customs, thousands of years old, were the same as those in vogue at the present day. What Mr. Lane says of the modern Egyptians is true of ancient times as well: "The natural liking of the Egyptians for music is shown by their habit of regulating their motions, and relieving the dulness of their occupations, in various labours, by songs or chants. Thus do the boatmen in rowing, etc., the peasants in raising water, the porters in carrying heavy weights with poles; men, boys, and girls, in assisting builders by bringing bricks, stones, and mortar, and removing rubbish; so also the sawyers, reapers, and many other labourers."[1] It is an interesting fact that the ancient Egyptians appear to have discerned some kind of connexion between nature and music, for, as is pointed out by Mr. Bosanquet,[2] they "perceived the distinction of the perfect intervals from others, and regarded them as typical of the seasons, spring bearing

[1] *An Account of the Manners and Customs of the Moder Egyptians*, ii. p. 59.

[2] *Encycl. Brit.* xvii. 78.

the proportion of a *fourth* to autumn, of a *fifth* to winter, and of an octave to summer."

Mr. Lane gives an example of a modern Egyptian melody[1] which, on examination, however, will be seen to be quite in the style of the primitive melodies given above; rhythm, tonality, and monotony are strongly marked; it will be noticed, too, that it is within the compass of a *fifth*:—

"Most of the popular airs of the Egyptians," says Mr. Lane, "though of a similar character, in most respects, to the music of their professional performers, are very simple, consisting of only a few notes which serve for every one or two lines of a song, and which are, therefore, repeated many times."[2]

Mr. Lane does not mention anything about harmony; but there would appear to be some grounds for believing that even amongst the ancient Egyptians, at all events among skilled professional musicians, some rudimentary elements of harmony were not unknown. Mr. Bosanquet says: "We have Egyptian paintings of the period of the fourth dynasty and Greek sculptures

[1] *Op. cit.* ii. p. 85. [2] *Op. cit.* ii. p. 50.

of players on pipes of different lengths which must have produced notes of different pitches; and sometimes the same party plays on string instruments with necks whereon two strings, differently stopped and yet sounded together, would have yielded a combination of different notes; and this, though a speechless, is a strong evidence that the musicians so represented made at least a forecast of modern harmony.[1]" Egypt was the country which originally gave the Greeks their music; and it was from the Egyptians that the Greeks imported a stringed instrument which had a bridge "placed under the strings, so that one-third of the entire length was on one side and two-thirds on the other; the shorter division when sounded was, of course, an octave higher than the longer; this was used by Anacreon (middle of sixth century B.C.) to accompany his singing; it was called a *Magadis* ('doubling bridge')."[2]

From the ancient Egyptian monuments we learn further, that music must have occupied an important place in the life of the people; the inscriptions tell us that musicians held high places at the Court; sacrifices were accompanied by music; dancing and music went together, as we should expect; and music was played at feasts. Music was also necessary at the burial of the dead, and the mourning for the departed consisted of instrumental as well as vocal music. One inscription gives a representation of the ceremony of mourning

[1] *Encycl. Brit.* xvii. 78. [2] *Ibid.*

for the dead; it takes place in the chamber of the dead, and harp-players, singers, and dancers are represented.[1]

On Egyptian musical instruments, see Ambros, *Op. cit.* pp. 346 ff., Forkel, *Op. cit.* i. pp. 72 ff. 99; Riehm, *Handwörterbuch des Biblischen Altertums*, art. "Musik"; and the art. "Musik" in the *Encycl. Bibl.*

§ IV. *Music among the Assyrians.*

We have, it appears, a good deal to learn yet about the place music occupied among the Assyrians; for, while our knowledge of the subject is very limited, there are certain indications which suggest that the Assyrians had some distinctly advanced ideas regarding music. The fact, for example, that a different musical tone was believed to have first emanated from each of the seven planets[2] points to a somewhat developed musical conception. From the sculptures which adorned the palace of Sennacherib[3] we learn that music, both vocal and instrumental, contributed to the glorification of the Assyrian kings. One inscription represents women singing and clapping their hands at the same time; this points again to the important place occupied by the rhythmical element. Another inscription supplies us with a detail of particular interest, a

[1] For illustrations of this kind, see Rosellini, *Les Monumens de l'Egypte et de la Nubie*, Pl. xciv. fig. 2, Pl. xcvi. fig. 6. Lepsius, *Denkmäler aus Aegypten und Aethiopien*, Div. ii. Pl. 52, 53.

[2] *Cp.* Jeremias, *Das alte Testament im Lichte des alten Orients*, p. 334 (1904).

[3] Situated near the present village of Koujundjik.

woman is depicted singing with her hand at her throat; this is characteristically oriental, and is constantly to be seen at the present day among Persian and Arabian women; it is done in order to enable the singer to bring out a shrill and vibrating tone.[1] This is another instance of the continuance to the present time of customs which have been in vogue for millenniums. That music among the Assyrians was used for religious as well as secular purposes is proved by the fact that on various inscriptions there are representations of sacrifices being accompanied by music. Important for the history of music among the people of Judah, is an inscription from the palace of Asshurbanipal,[2] which tells, among other things, of how the Assyrian king took captive from Hezekiah, King of Judah, both male and female musicians; the inscription thus witnesses to the existence of music in Jerusalem[3] in pre-exilic times, and the fact is not without importance regarding the question of the Temple music before the Exile. Another item of interest, for it illustrates a practice of which mention is made in both the Old and New Testaments, is the allusion to music and singing in the mourning for the dead; thus, it is said that at the funeral of an Assyrian king, women wailed when all the mourners had assembled; elsewhere it is said that "the wives (of

[1] Ambros, *Op. cit.* p. 388. [2] 668-626 B.C.

[3] The context in the inscription states definitely that the musicians, together with other captives, were taken from Hezekiah's palace in Jerusalem to Asshurbanipal.

the deceased) mourned, and the friends made response" (*Cp.* also Jer. xlviii. 36-38; 2 Chron. xxxv. 25; 2 Macc. iii. 19 ff; 2 Macc. i. 18, 19; Mark v. 38).

§ V. *Music among the ancient Greeks.*

It has been most truly said, in reference to music among the nations of antiquity, that "it is a fact which is seen to recur among all races that a period of artistic production never runs simultaneously with a period of the development of theory. The artist produces, but he does not reflect upon what he has brought forth."[1] In no instance is this more true than in that of the ancient Greeks; much, very much, was produced before Aristotle, and his pupil, Aristoxenus, taught, in truly wonderful style, their theory of music. Aristoxenus was the first to explain, on scientific lines, the difference between melody and rhythm in music; he taught that "*Melos* is all that is concerned with the varying quality of tones such as is conditioned by their high or low pitch, both in reference to melody and accompaniment. Rhythm, on the other hand, is the quantitative difference in time of consecutive tones."[2] He observes that there are two kinds of *Melos*, the *Melos* of that which is sung, and the *Melos* of that which is spoken; from this it is clear that already in the fourth century B.C.[3] the difference between cantilla-

[1] B. von Sokolowsky, *Die Musik des griechischen Alterthums und des Orients*, in A. W. Ambros' *Geschichte der Musik*, p. 35 (1887).

[2] Quoted by von Sokolowsky, *Op. cit.* p. 37.

[3] Aristoxenus lived in the latter part of the fourth century B.C.

tion and melody proper must have long been recognised among the Greeks; and this fact is perhaps not without some bearing upon what the style and character of the music must have been in the Jewish Temple during the two centuries immediately preceding the beginning of the Christian era; for already previous to these centuries the influence of the Greek spirit had become very marked upon the Jewish nation, while at the commencement of the second century B.C., under the Seleucid rule, this influence was greatly increased, Hellenic thought and culture being pressed upon the nation from without, but also welcomed by the nation from within.[1] The protest against this influence which culminated in the Maccabæan struggle was not aimed so much against Hellenic culture as against the deliberate attempt on the part of Antiochus Epiphanes[2] to root out the Jewish religion. The presumption seems justified that the influence of Greek culture manifested itself in the domain of music as well as in other directions (though it must be confessed that actual *data* on the subject are wanting), and if so, then it is more than probable that the music in the Temple-worship was developed in accordance with it.

But, as already pointed out in the opening words of this section, there was a period of production before the period of the development of theory began, and we are not without some indications as to what the character

[1] See *e.g.* i. Macc. i. 11-15, ii. Macc. iv. 7-15, etc.

[2] He reigned from 175-164 B.C.

of these musical productions must have been. One fact of prime importance is that, even in a comparatively speaking advanced stage of Greek music, the number of tones available was small. "In the development of European scales," says Dr. Myers, "it would be rash to suppose that the octave has always been the distance theoretically subjected to division. The earliest Greek melodies, for example, appear to have had a much narrower compass. The tetrachord is thought to have been the first attempt at a scale in Greece. It consisted of the interval of a fourth divided into three parts. Another added tetrachord subsequently completed the octave. The mode of construction of the particular scales is found to vary widely among different peoples, and even among the same people at different times and in different kinds of music. Most usually the octave of the particular scales is divided into five or seven tones. The five-toned or pentatonic scale occurs in every continent. A common form of it, found, for example, in Chinese, Japanese, and Scottish music, omits the fourth and the seventh. . ."[1] The origin of the pentatonic scale is not known.

A few specimens of ancient Greek music have been discovered; the first of these to be brought to light were three hymns, to Apollo, Nemesis, and Calliope respectively; they were first discovered by Vincentio Galilei; he got them from a rich Florentine, who had copied them carefully from a manuscript in the library

[1] *Op. cit.* pp. 241 f.

of Cardinal St. Angelo, in Rome; they were first published in 1581. A copy of them was found later among the papers of Archbishop Ussher, and published in 1672.[1] The date of these is some time during the second century A.D.,[2] though an earlier date has been claimed for them.[3] A few bars of one of these hymns, that to Nemesis, may be given; it is ascribed to Mesomedes, who lived during the reign of the Emperor Hadrian.[4] The following portion of the hymn is taken from Janus:—[5]

"Apparently the Greeks employed different modes[6] [*i.e.*, scales] according to the metre chosen, and they

[1] See Forkel, *Op. cit.* I. p. 421; he gives all three hymns in full on pp. 427 ff.

[2] D.B. Monro, *The Modes of Ancient Greek Music*, p. 87 (1894).

[3] R. H. M. Bosanquet, *Encycl. Brit.*, xvii. 79.

[4] 117-138 A.D.

[5] Carolus Janus, *Musici Scriptores Græci*, Supplementum Melodiarum, Reliquiæ, pp. 55 ff. (in *Bibliotheca Scriptorum Græcorum et Romanorum Teubneriana*, Leipzig, 1889).

[6] Corresponding to the modern major and minor modes.

came to attach broad distinguishing characteristics to each of the modes.[1] The Dorian mode, for example, was reputed to be severe and virile, others to be smooth, erotic, suitable for boys, and so forth. But writers differ so much in their attitude to the various modes that it is impossible to lay much stress on their opinions."[2] Another specimen, written in the Ionian mode, was found by Mr. R. H. Ramsay on a gravestone near Tralles; it professes to have been written by one Seikelos; the words of the inscription are written in larger character than the "notes," and the discovery that the small letters between the lines were musical notes was made by Dr. Wessely.[3] The following transcription into modern notation is from Monro, *Op. cit.* p. 89:—

[1] The more important are: The Lydian, Mixolydian, Syntonolydian, Ionian, Phrygian, Aeolian, and Dorian.

[2] Myers, *Op. cit.* p. 243. Monro, *Op. cit.* p. 133.

One other example, for which greater antiquity is claimed, must be referred to. "The most ancient connected specimen of music which we have is the famous Greek pæan to Apollo in the Phrygian scale of the Doric mode, which was discovered at Delphi in 1893 by the members of the French School of Archæology at Athens[1] . . . . it is in the regulation five-time peculiar to the pæan, and is undoubtedly very ancient, although it may be doubted whether the air is as old as 277 B.C., the date of the establishment of the Soteria Festival, at which it was sung." The ode was accompanied by the flute and the *kithara*.[2] The following few bars of it may be added :—

These examples, it must be remembered, are specimens of Greek music at times when this had been greatly developed, and when performed must have had an entirely different effect from that gained by playing them or singing them as they now stand. We know very little about the time at which they were taken,

[1] *Révue des Études Grecques*, vii. 5 f.

[2] *Encycl. Bibl.*, iii. p. 3242.

and we cannot state with absolute certainty the value of the different notes; moreover, we have very slight knowledge regarding the kind of harmonies used in Greek music, but that they cannot have been unpleasant may be gathered from the words of Aristotle when describing what he calls antiphonal singing. He says that it is the singing of a melody by men an octave lower than is being sung by boys, and that this is the only perfect interval which is allowable in singing together, the other perfect intervals, the fourth and the fifth, being excluded.[1] This prohibition almost compels one to suppose that the singing together of other intervals was not unknown, in which case it is fair to assume that the result was not a "Kakomusia," as Aristides calls the music of the Phœnicians.[2] At any rate, the advanced stage which music had reached among the Greeks in the fourth century B.C., and the influence which Hellenic culture had upon the Jews, are facts which must be taken into consideration in seeking to gain an insight into the character of the music of the Temple-worship as this existed during the two or three centuries immediately preceding the Christian era, up to the time of the destruction of Jerusalem in 70 A.D.

VI. *Music among the Arabs.*

Finally, we must try and gather a few *data* regarding music among the Arabs; this is particularly important,

[1] R. H. Bosanquet, *Op. cit.* xvii. 79. [2] Ambros, *Op. cit.* p. 395.

because the Arabs have in so many respects retained customs and manners which go back to a high antiquity,[1] that in respect of music, too, it is very probable that present-day practice has retained much that is ancient. On the other hand, there seems no doubt at all that among some classes of Arabs there has been considerable development; this is seen, apart from other indications, in the fact that the mediæval Arabs employed musical notation, and in certain of the more modern Arabic music a heptatonic scale is used. "Arabian theorists included quarter-tones in the scales which they constructed, and it has been stated that in Syria a scale occurs consisting of equally tempered quarter-tones. The various quarter- and third-tone scales described by Arabian and other writers are probably always general scales; they are rarely, if ever, particular or instrumental scales. When quarter-tone intervals occur in any piece of Arabic music, the notes concerned are only grace notes, or play an otherwise unimportant part in the melody."[2] It seems clear that among the Arabs, then, two musical stages are to be discerned—an advanced and a primitive one; it is, of course, only the latter that at present interests us.[3] In this earlier type of music it is rarely that the compass of notes in a melody reaches five;

[1] *Cp.* Conder, *Tent Work in Palestine*, p. 332 (1889).

[2] Myers, *Op. cit.* p. 245. *cp.* Forkel, *Op. cit.* i. 426.

[3] It is worth noting that the ancient world ascribed much in the way of musical invention to the Arabs, see Forkel, *Op. cit.* i. 426.

that is evidently a trace of ancient times. Another point of interest is that in the early form of music harmony is unknown among modern Arabs; Benzinger tells that when Egyptian or Turkish military bands play their own oriental tunes all the instruments play in unison.[1] It will give us some insight into the music of the Arabs, and the effect it has upon European listeners, if we quote from the impressions of the three well-known travellers, Niebuhr, Lane, and Thomson. The first of these speaks of the love that all Arabs have for music, and how widely it is practised; he says that for every respectable Turk or Arab it would be considered unfitting not to understand music and dancing. When he says, further, that "neither in Egypt, Arabia, or India was I able to discover that they understood how to put a melody on paper," he shows that he is giving us an account of the music of the people, *i.e.* of the primitive, traditional form; for it is well-known that both Indian and Arabian theorists had a system of notation;[2] but he speaks also of a different type of music of which mention will be made in a moment. It is, again, probably, traditional melody which is referred to when he says: "I have often heard sheikhs sing a passage out of the Koran which I liked well on account of the natural kind of music, for they never forced their voices in the effort to

[1] See his art. on "Musik" in Hauck's *Realencyklopädie für Protestantische Theologie und Kirche.*

[2] Myers, *Op. cit.* p. 240,

sing too high."[1] He tells, further, of how he heard some sailors singing their love-songs, and says: "The melodies of all their songs were different, one of the singers who took the part of leader, sang one line, then the others repeated the same words and the same melody three, four, or five tones lower, this was done line by line to the end; they kept time by clapping their hands as they had no drum." That this must have represented a later stage of musical development than that represented by the singing of the sheikhs, just mentioned, seems evident from the fact of more than one part having been sung simultaneously; sailors were the most likely people of all to have come under the influence of other than native music. In speaking of oriental music generally, Niebuhr says: "The melodies of all orientals are solemn and simple. It is demanded of all singers that they sing so distinctly that every word can be understood." He says, finally (in spite of what was said just now), that when several instruments and voices play or sing together, it is always done in unison.[2]

Next, Mr. Lane writes as follows: "The most remarkable peculiarity in the Arab system of music is the division of tones into thirds . . . these small and delicate gradations of sound give a peculiar softness to the performances of Arab musicians, which are generally of a plaintive character."[3] Like Niebuhr, he

[1] The same melody would be sung on a variety of occasions, *cp.* p. 6.

[2] *Reisebeschreibung nach Arabien und andern umliegenden Ländern*, i. pp. 175 ff. (1774).

[3] *Op. cit.* ii. p. 60.

evidently found the music of the Arabs not unpleasant to the ear. Mr. W. M. Thomson, on the other hand, thinks differently; in speaking of the public music he had heard in Damascus, he says: "The music was excruciating, and the singing the most outrageous concert of harsh, nasal sounds I ever heard. The same nasal twang and grating gutturals is heard in all the singing of every denomination throughout the East. The Orientals know nothing of harmony, and cannot appreciate it when heard, but they are often spellbound or wrought up to transports of ecstasy by that very music which has tortured your nerves. I have rarely known song to be more truly effective than among these stolid children of the East, especially in such places of public resort. Seated on a raised platform at one end of the coffee-shop, half-a-dozen performers discourse strange music from curious instruments, interspersed occasionally with wild bursts of song, which seem to electrify the smoking, coffee-sipping company. They usually have a violin, two or three kinds of flutes, a tambourine, kettle-drums, and a derbekkeh. One man plays a large harp, lying upon his lap, called a kânûn, and an expert performer often makes very agreeable music with it . . . There are also players on the guitar, or kamanjeh, and one of them has a very large instrument of that kind, over whose few chords his nimble fingers sweep at times like magic."[1] This is an interesting account, but it will

[1] *The Land and the Book* (Lebanon, Damascus, and beyond Jordan), pp. 392 f. (1886).

be obvious at once that it is modern oriental music which has been described; it is a good illustration of the truth that two types of music exist at the present day among the Arabs, which must be sharply differentiated; this is not difficult to do when one remembers the prime characteristics of the early type. But it is a striking fact how in some respects the primitive is mixed up with the more developed; for example, the old-world derbekkeh (practically a tom-tom), with the chord-producing kamanjeh. But it bears out what Dr. Myers says, that "there is hardly any other branch of ethnology where so much remains to be done, and where the opportunities for research are so rapidly vanishing beyond recall, as the study of comparative music. The borrowing and adulteration of music proceed apace. When tribes, formerly hostile, become pacified, fresh routes are opened up for the mutual exchange and contamination of different styles of primitive music. When sacred and profane European tunes are introduced by the missionary or the trader, unpolluted aboriginal music soon has a precarious existence. We have evidence of these conditions in the influence of Arabic or Portuguese tunes introduced into Africa, and in the spread of favourite native airs throughout North America and throughout Australia."[1] We shall have to refer again to the music of the Arabs in the next chapter.

[1] *Op. cit.* p. 236.

* * * * * *

Although the above *data* offer little more than a glimpse into the subjects concerned, it is, nevertheless, possible and permissible to draw some conclusions from them regarding music and song among the Israelites. This must be the subject of our next two chapters.

CHAPTER II.

MUSIC AMONG THE ISRAELITES.

IN the preceding chapter certain *data* have been brought together concerning music among a variety of different peoples. From these *data* one is justified in drawing some conclusions regarding the character of music among the Israelites. While it is fully realized that there is a certain precariousness in forming conclusions which are based solely on analogy, there is this to be said in justification for doing so, namely, that there is no alternative. We have but few *data* in the Old Testament regarding the character of Israelite music; certain inferences of a general kind may be drawn, no doubt, but as to the manner of singing, the kind of melodies, their structure and compass, etc., etc., we are almost wholly in the dark if we have to rely solely on the Old Testament. We are, therefore, thrown upon the argument from analogy; and, as will be seen, in the present case at all events, this method can be used with a good deal of force.

§ I. *The Primitive Period.*

In the preceding chapter we dealt, first of all,

with music among uncultured peoples; we were able to gather here the following definite facts, among others:—

In the music of peoples in a not very advanced stage of culture there are certain characteristics which are invariably manifested; since this is always seen to be the case, the inference seems justified that the earliest form of music among the Hebrews was similar in these fundamental characteristics to that of other races in a corresponding stage of civilisation. For example, the earliest stage of which we have any echoes, as far as the Hebrews are concerned, is the nomadic; we know something about the music of peoples who are still, of others who have been, in the nomadic stage, and on the analogy of what we know of the music of these, we may, with some show of reason, claim to know something about the music of the Hebrews in the nomadic stage, so far as these fundamental characteristics are concerned. First and foremost among these is the predominance of the rhythmical element over all else. "Singing" was originally, above all things, rhythmical declamation. Here it is worth while to draw attention again to the music of the Arabs,[1] especially as in Arabia and in parts of Syria, these are still in the nomadic stage; and all authorities are agreed that the nomadic Arabs of to-day are in all essentials what they have been for milleniums.

[1] We refer, of course, to the primitive music of the Arabs, not to its later development; *cp.* what was said on . 28.

Benzinger holds, without doubt rightly, that, speaking generally, we must picture ancient Hebrew music to ourselves as corresponding largely to that of the modern Arabs. "It would," he says, "be a grievous error to despise this latter, because it does not appeal to our ears—*i.e.* because our ears are not accustomed to it—and because it knows nothing of harmony. With the same right the Orientals regard our beautiful harmonious music as a dreadful noise."[1] But it is one of the main characteristics of Arab music that rhythmical accentuation is the most important element; to quote Benzinger again; "For the proper estimation of both ancient Hebrew and modern oriental music, one must above all realize that with both, rhythm plays an exceedingly important *rôle* at the cost of melody."[2] The rhythmical element is still the dominant one in Arab folk-songs which are sung at the present day; and there can be little doubt that these folk-songs, at any rate in their musical structure, go back to a great antiquity. It is well known that in early forms of song two accompanying actions usually assisted in marking the rhythm, namely, the playing of the drum, and dancing; it is interesting, therefore, to find that in what may certainly be regarded as an echo of the kind of music which obtained among the Hebrews while still in the nomadic stage, these

[1] Art. "Musik," in Hauck's *Realencyklopädie fur Protestanische Theologie und Kirche*, xiii. 599.

[2] *Ibid.*

two accompanying actions are mentioned in connexion with song. After the "Song of Moses" in Exod. vi. 1-18, we read in verse 20: "*And Miriam the prophetess, the sister of Aaron, took a timbrel in her hand; and all the women went out after her with timbrels and with dances.*" The Hebrew word for "timbrel" is *tôph*, probably the most primitive musical instrument among the Hebrews; it would be better described as a hand-drum, or tom-tom; it was "simply a ring of wood or metal, covered with a tightly drawn skin, occasionally provided with small pieces of metal hung around the rim, exactly like those on the modern tambourine, of which the *tôph* was the prototype. The instrument was held up in one hand and struck with the other."[1]

But where rhythmical accentuation plays this leading part in music, two things are almost certain to follow—they do follow in every case that has been observed—melody is subordinated, and there is but the scantiest, if any, feeling for harmony; indeed, melody, in the music of the early Hebrews (judging from the analogy of the Arabs), could better be described as a kind of declamatory recitative; while harmony, if such existed at all in the early stage of which we are thinking (which is exceedingly doubtful, for the modern Arabs know no harmony) would, at the outside, have consisted in the singing or playing of two parts, one an octave lower

[1] J. D. Prince, in *Encycl. Bibl.* iii. 3226.

than the other.[1] Again, when so little stress was laid on melody, it is an obvious inference to suppose that its compass was very limited, in other words, that only a few notes were made use of, and that the intervals were small. Indeed, that melodies had not many tones, and were of limited compass, is proved by what we know of primitive musical instruments; stringed instruments and flutes had in ancient times very few tones; the two earliest forms of harps of which we have record on inscriptions cannot possibly have had many notes. It is in the highest degree improbable that the ancient Hebrews would have had musical instruments of a more elaborate kind than those, for example, of the Egyptians or Assyrians; everything points the other way. We shall probably be not far wrong in saying that a compass of four notes was very rare in ancient Hebrew melody; three notes is more likely to have been the extent of the compass. Then, once more, where so little importance was attached to melody, there were not likely to have been many melodies in existence; and, therefore, one melody would serve for the words of different songs. This is borne out by the fact that even in much later times ancient melodies were utilized for more than one song.[2] From the analogy of the music of other peoples, we may assume

[1] This is often, though quite erroneously, spoken of as "singing in unison"; to sing in unison the two parts must sing the same note together; if one part is sung an octave lower than the other, that is not singing in unison, but in harmony—the simplest form of harmony, it is true.

[2] See, on this, p. 74.

that early Hebrew melodies, and the same is probably true of post-exilic times, were very short, consisting probably of not more than two of what we should call bars nowadays; from this it follows that a melody must have been repeated over and over again in singing a song. We shall see presently that there is another reason which justifies the assumption that Hebrew melodies were very short. There is one more element in the music of the Arabs which must be taken into consideration in trying to gain some insight into the character of ancient Hebrew music; we give, in substance, the words of Benzinger (and the judgment of most travellers is the same concerning the music of the Arabs): in the first place, all tones are played and sung "out of tune," according to our judgment (generally speaking, they play and sing in a minor key);[1] but it is certain that their playing and singing out of tune is not due to what we should call a "bad ear," because their mode of playing and singing is "constant"; and they maintain, moreover, that Europeans play and sing out of tune. In the second place, their intervals are different from ours, which they regard as unmusical; their intervals are of a different character from those of European music, they are smaller, and consequently more in number. "This has not taken place," says Benzinger, "in Christian times; it is ancient; and one may say with certainty that the same obtained among the ancient Hebrews."

[1] This is also the case, as a rule, among other peoples of limited culture.

Apart, however, from what may be reasonably inferred from analogy, it is evident from the Old Testament that the old Hebrews loved music; their tradition that Jubal was the father of music (Gen. iv. 21)[1] shows that the use of instrumental music, still more so then in the case of song, was very ancient; and this is borne out by such passages as Exod. xv. 20, Judges ix. 27, xxi. 21, which re-echo conditions of life in the more or less nomadic stage.

§ II. *The Davidic Period.*

In the next place, we drew attention in the preceding chapter to a few details about the music of the ancient Egyptians. This is important from our present point of view, because we know the influence of Egypt upon the Israelites to have been very marked at certain periods of their history; and that this influence was exercised in the domain of musical culture, as well as in other respects, is a reasonable assumption. The period during which Egyptian influence was most likely to have been felt by the inhabitants of Palestine coincides more or less with the establishment of the monarchy. Of course this influence had been exercised in earlier times as well (*e.g.* during the Tell-el Amarna period)[2]; but it is probable that it was more far-reaching in its effects

[1] *Cp.* the Egyptian tradition that their holiest melodies originated from Isis, and the Assyrian belief that musical tones first emanated from the planets; *cp.* also the Greek Muses.

[2] 14th cen. B.C.

when settled life among the Israelites had taken the place of the conditions which had prevailed during earlier periods, such, for example, as that which immediately preceded the establishment of monarchy, namely, during that of the so-called Judges. It is not without interest that the new era in the domain of music among the Israelites, inaugurated by David, should have more or less coincided with the renewal of more intimate relationships between Egypt and Palestine. That the name of David is rightly connected with a development of music among the Israelites as universally recognized, though authorities may differ as to the actual *rôle* that David played in this development. And that there was closer intercourse between Egyptians and Israelites not long after the time of David is certain; our records are scanty as to details, but of the main fact there can be no doubt. That the Israelites were helped by the Egyptians in their wars against the Philistines is distinctly stated in 1 Kings ix. 16; "*Pharaoh king of Egypt had gone up, and taken Gezer,*[1] *and burnt it with fire, and slain the Canaanites that dwelt in the city, and given it for a portion unto his daughter, Solomon's wife.*" This union between the two royal families points to a close intercourse between the two nations. Professor Müller says: "About 950, one

[1] That Gezer had hitherto been in the possession of the Philistines is clear from 2 Sam. v. 25, where it is mentioned as the limit of David's pursuit of these; it was on the border of the Philistine territory.

family of Libyan officers had become so influential, that they could venture to put one of themselves upon the throne, Sosenk I. This Pharaoh, the contemporary of Solomon and his son, who reigned at least twenty-one years, was more energetic, and again exercised influence upon Syria. He seems to have assisted Israel against the Philistines."[1] The information, though scanty, is sufficient to show that renewed and close intercourse between Israel and Egypt took place not long after the opening of a new era in the history of music among the Israelites. The belief is, therefore, an entirely reasonable one, that at this period the development of Israelite music received a further impetus from the influence of Egypt. It is known that in later days a similar influence on the part of Egypt was exercised upon the music of the Greeks.[2]

In what precise details Egyptian influence at this period is likely to have affected the music of the Israelites is obviously a question impossible to answer; the *fact* that such an influence was exercised is, as we have seen, almost inevitable; but as to the details, we are wholly in the dark. All that can be said is that, in view of the comparatively advanced state of Egyptian civilisation, musical culture must have been considerably more developed among the Egyptians than among the Israelites, and therefore the effect of Egyptian influence upon the music of the Israelites must have

[1] *Encycl. Bibl.* ii. 1243. [2] See p. 18.

been in the direction of developing and improving it. This is the more likely to have been the case because, what one may call the Davidic school, had been the means of preparing a receptive soil. "The *rôle* which singing and music played in the second Temple, and the place taken up by singers and musicians in the *personnel* of the Temple, is only comprehensible on the supposition that music had a definite place in the Temple-worship *before* the Exile. And when tradition traces all this back to David, and makes him the real founder of the Temple music, it is not mere phantasy which has spun itself out of the early indications of David's proficiency in musical art. It is in the nature of things highly probable that the King who clearly took great delight in music, and who had at his court his men and women singers, his musicians and dancers, should have employed these in worship as well."[1]

§ III. *The Post-exilic Period.*

It is probable that when the Israelites returned from the Exile they brought with them the seeds of further development in the domain of music. By saying this it is not intended to imply that the music of Babylonia and Assyria was of a more developed character than that of Egypt; what is meant is that during the seventy years of Captivity the Israelites must have been frequent witnesses of the elaborate ritual of Baby-

[1] Benzinger, *Op. cit.* p. 598.

lonian worship, in which music played a considerable part, and that this actual seeing and hearing must have been deeper and more lasting in its effect than that of the Egyptian music during the earlier period; the difference was, roughly speaking, that between actually hearing and hearing about. In the forms of the musical instruments depicted on Babylonian-Assyrian and Egyptian monuments there is great similarity; the music of these nations must, therefore, have been similar in many essential points; and the influence under which the Israelites came, in this respect, during the Exile was rather to emphasize and drive home something with which they were already to some extent familiar. A small, though not altogether unimportant, indication of Babylonian interest in music during the Exile is afforded in Psalm cxxxvii.,[1] where the singing of Jehovah's songs (*i.e.* songs which had been part of the Temple-worship) is mentioned in connexion with the playing of harps—at least, this is the implication; the refusal of the captives to do so does not disprove the fact that their oppressors desired to hear these songs. Attention must also be called again to the inscription of Asshurbanipal, mentioned above, as showing that

[1] Cheyne (*The Origin and Religious Contents of the Psalter*, p. 70) places this psalm "in the time of Simon the Maccabee"; Briggs (*The Book of Psalms*, I. p. lxxxix.) assigns it to the period of the Exile. There does not seem sufficient reason for denying this latter date to the psalm; on the other hand, it will be granted that it is extremely probable that all the earlier psalms have been "worked over" by later redactors; this must have presented itself as a duty very often.

there must have been a good deal for Babylonian influence to work upon.[1] After the Exile we are told of numerous singers and musicians who returned with Zerubbabel. This may be taken as pointing to a two-fold truth; it proves, on the one hand, that the tradition regarding the Temple music was not lost, but was preserved and handed down (*cp.* Psalm cxxxvii.); and, on the other hand, it may be taken to show that Babylonian influence upon the music of the Israelites was a real factor in the development of the latter. In connexion with what has just been said, the following passages should be consulted: Ezra ii. 41, iii. 10 ff., vi. 8 ff., vii. 20 ff.; Neh. vii. 44, xi. 22, 23, xii. 28, 37 ff. 47, xiii. 10.

Just as a new era in the history of Israelite music was opened soon after the establishment of the monarchy—which, for convenience' sake, may be termed the Davidic Era—during which Egyptian influence made a mark on the national music, so after the Exile another era was opened, the Post-exilic Era, during which the results of Babylonian influence had a further effect upon the national music. In this Post-exilic Era, there were, we may believe, in the music of the people melodies in the stricter sense; but here, too, declamation caused the melody to be subordinated. We get some clue as to the structure of melody from the Hebrew text of the Psalms. Here the strophes and verses are uneven as regards the number of words and syllables; the melody must, therefore, have been

[1] See p. 20.

variable in the sense that some notes were longer and some shorter in different verses. From the analogy of other early music, we are justified in taking it for granted that Hebrew melodies were not long. Moreover, the fact that some psalms were sung antiphonally makes it highly probable that the same melody went to each verse, or for several verses in succession; for indications as to the antiphonal singing of some psalms, see Jer. xxxiii. 2, Ezra iii. 2, and especially 1 Sam. xviii. 7, Ps. cvi. 48, cxviii. 1-14, 29, cxxxvi. (*cp.* also the Hebrew psalm appended to the Hebrew of Ecclesiasticus li. 12; this is, in structure, based on Ps. cxxxvi.). Benzinger thinks that the melody was sung to each half-verse, possibly to each verse, and was repeated over and over again for each half-verse or verse; and that, therefore, this melody must have varied in the length of its different notes because of the various lengths of the verses; he points to present-day use among the Arabs as supporting this view. In general he holds, with regard to the character of Hebrew music during the Post-exilic period, that we must strike a mean between the exaggerated praise bestowed upon it in the Talmud, and the contemptuous estimate which would class it as quite beneath notice, and which would regard it simply as a barbaric noise.

§ IV. *The Greek Period.*

Finally, there is one other stage in the history of music among the Israelites which must be mentioned, that, namely, during which it is to be supposed that the influence of Greek music played some part in the development of Hebrew music. It must be confessed that we have no direct *data* upon which to base this supposition other than the probability of the case; but the influence of Hellenic culture upon the Jews during the two last centuries B.C., referred to in the preceding chapter, makes it very probable that, to some extent, Greek music influenced that of the Jews. It is certain that in this period the taste for music of a secular kind increased greatly; this is graphically brought out by Ben-Sira, who seems to have been a great lover of music (see Ecclus. xxxii. 3-6, xl. 20, 21); and it is improbable that sacred music remained untouched if the general taste for music had increased. Ben-Sira refers with evident satisfaction to the Temple music when he says:—

> "And they sang the song with their voice,
> Yea, to the music they uttered a joyful strain."[1]
> (see Ecclus. l. 18, *cp.* l. 16)

This increased taste for music can scarcely be unconnected with the Hellenizing movement.[2]

It would seem, then, that, roughly speaking, the history of music among the Israelites can be divided into four periods, viz.:—

[1] According to the Hebrew text, emended.

[2] *Cp.* also the Aramaicized Greek names of musical instruments in the book of Daniel; see p. 52.

The "Primitive" Period.

The Davidic Period.

The Post-exilic Period.

The Hellenistic Period.

In the first of these the characteristics of Israelite music did not, presumably, differ from those of the music of other peoples in the nomadic stage. In the second, an indigenous development was influenced and furthered by the music of the Egyptians. In the third, Assyro-Babylonian influence assisted in this development; and in the fourth, Greek music helped still further in the development and improvement of Israelite music.

CHAPTER III.

INSTRUMENTAL MUSIC AMONG THE ISRAELITES.

§ I. *Instruments used by the Israelites.*

FROM one point of view instrumental music among the Israelites played an altogether subordinate part, for it was never regarded as anything but an accompaniment to the singing. But this instrumental accompaniment tended to become more and more elaborate, so that it ultimately assumed a place of great importance in the Temple worship, and especially during the singing of the Psalms. This fact makes it advisable that we should gain some definite ideas about the musical instruments in use among the Israelites. These can be divided into three classes:—

(*a*) *Instruments of percussion.* These represent the most primitive type of musical instruments; and the earliest form of them was the *Tôph*, or "Drum" (*cp.* 1 Sam. x. 5, xviii. 6; 1 Chron. xiii. 8; Ps. lxviii. 26, lxxxi. 3, cxlix. 3, cl. 4; Is. v. 12, etc., etc.). A modification of this is seen in the *Zelzelim*, "Cymbals," *i.e.* something that makes a clashing sound (*cp.* 2 Sam. vi. 5; 1 Chron. xiii. 8; Ps. cl. 5); closely connected with these were the *Meziltaim*, also translated "Cymbals" (both words come from the same Hebrew root), and sometimes mentioned together with the preceding (*cp.* 2 Sam. vi. 5; 1 Chron. xiii. 8, xv. 19, 28, xxv. 1-6; 2 Chron. v. 12, 13; Ezra iii. 10; Neh. xii. 27, etc.). It is difficult to determine the character of another ancient instrument, the *Shalishim*, mentioned in connexion with the drum in 1 Sam. xviii. 6 (its only occurrence in the Old Testament); its name implies that it had something to do with "three" things, but what these were is a difficult question to answer. The fact that this instrument was used by the women who came out to meet David returning from the slaughter of the Philistines, shows that it was in use among the common people, and that, therefore, like the drum, it must have been a simple instrument requiring no skill to play. As it was evidently a somewhat primitive instrument, the "three" cannot refer to different-sounding tones, and therefore the idea of its being a three-stringed instrument (R.V. marg.) is very improbable; for the same reason its seems unlikely that it corresponded to the Egyptian *sistrum*. The suggestion may be hazarded that it was a form of drum, differing from this in having the skin drawn over three pieces of stick fixed together in triangular shape. This would be easier to construct than the circle-shaped *Tôph*. One other instrument belongs to the percussion class, the *Mena'ane'im* (only mentioned in 2 Sam. vi. 5); the root from which this word comes means "to shake," and it may therefore represent something in the shape of a "rattle," thus corresponding to the Egyptian *sistrum* which, among the Egyptians, was "a small metal frame with loose metal bars carrying loose rings, borne and *swung* or *shaken* in the hand";[1] among the early Israelities it was presumably of a less elaborate charact er.

(*b*) *Wind Instruments.* The most primitive of these was the *Shôfar*,[2] "Ram's-horn," which is synonymous with *Keren*, "Horn" (*cp.* Josh. vi. 5; 1 Chron. xxv. 5; Ps. xlvii. 6, xcviii. 6, cl. 3, etc.). *Chazôzerah* was the "Trumpet," in the more modern sense (*cp.* Num. x. 2, xxxi. 6; 1 Chron. xv. 24, xvi. 42; 2 Chron. v. 12 f., vii. 6, xxix. 26 f.; 2 Kings xi. 14; Hosea v. 8; Ecclus. l. 16 ff.). Another instrument belonging to very early times was the *Chalil*, also called *Nechilah*, "Flute." This had originally only one note, like the two instruments just mentioned; but, later on, holes were bored in the flute, thus giving two or three notes, which in course of time were increased by making more holes. The earliest Hebrew flute was made of reed; later of wood, and, still later, of metal and ivory. The '*Ugab* (*cp.* Gen. iv. 21; Ps. cl. 4) seems to have been "some development from the double flute, such as a mouth-organ or pan's-pipe";[3] it was, in all probability, the same instrument as the

[1] Oxford Hebrew Lexicon, *s.v.*

[2] The only instrument still in use in the modern Synagogue.

[3] *Encycl. Bibl.* iii. 3229.

Mashrôkitha (only in Dan. iii. 5, 7, 10, 15), from a root meaning "to whistle." Lastly, there is the *Sumpônya* or "Bag-pipe" (Dan. iii. 5, 15, called "Dulcimer" in the Revised Version, but "Bag-pipe" in the margin).

(*c*) *String Instruments.* These appear to have occupied the most important position of all instruments among the Hebrews, from the Davidic period onwards, a fact which points to a comparatively advanced musical taste. The general name for stringed instruments is *neginôth;* the verb *naggên* means "to play a stringed instrument" (*cp.* 1 Sam. xvi. 16 f. 28, xviii. 10; 2 Kings iii. 15; Ps. xxxiii. 3; Is. xxiii. 16; Ezek. xxxiii. 32, &c.). The word *zammêr*, which is so frequently used in the Psalms, implies, "singing with musical accompaniment," see Ps. lxxi. 22, cxliv. 9, "to sing with the accompaniment of the *Kinnor*" (*cp.* Amos vi. 5; 1 Chron. xvi. 42; 2 Chron. v. 13, vii. 6, xxxiv. 12). *Kinnor*, "lyre," *nebel*, "harp," are the only two stringed musical instruments mentioned in the Old Testament outside the Book of Daniel, where *kitharis* (iii. 5 ff.) = *kinnor*, *pesanterin* (iii. 5 ff.) = *nebel*, and *sabbekha* (iii. 5, 7, 10), "sackbut," also occur. The strings were made of sheep's gut; the metal strings used by modern Arabs were, of course, unknown.

§ II. *Data concerning instrumental accompaniment to the Psalms.*

We have in various passages in the Old Testament,

and especially in the Psalms, a number of miscellaneous *data* regarding music and song among the Israelites; in the majority of cases these give us some insight into the musical accompaniment of the Psalms. Some of these passages we must now draw attention to, though to deal with them exhaustively is not our intention.

In the first place, whatever the character of Hebrew music from the point of view of western ideas, it is certain that it exercised often a striking effect upon its hearers (see *e.g.* Sam. xvi. 16 ff.,; 2 Kings iii. 15). We get an indication of another kind in Amos v. 22, 23, where we read: "*Yea, though ye offer me your burnt-offerings and meal-offerings, I will not accept them: neither will I regard the peace-offerings of your fat beasts. Take thou away from me the voice of thy songs; for I will not hear the melody of thy viols.*" The mention here together of sacrifices with songs and music suggests a close connexion between them; indeed, there is no reason to doubt that what we know to have been the case in later days happened also in the time of Amos, namely, that certain psalms were sung during the offering-up of sacrifices; this must greatly have enhanced the solemnity of the sacrificial rite. Then, in reference to rather later times, we read in Is. xxx. 29: "*Ye shall have a song, as in the night when a holy feast is kept; and gladness of heart, as when one goeth with a pipe to come into the mountain of the Lord.*" The instrumental accompaniment to song, clearly sacred song, which is implied in these two passages, is explicitly expressed in Is. xxxviii. 20: "*The Lord is ready to save me, therefore we will sing my songs to the stringed instruments all the days of our life in the house of the Lord.*"[1]

One clear indication of the relation between the singing and the accompaniment is given in 2 Chronicles, v. 13: "*The trumpeters and singers were as one, to make one sound to be heard in praising aud thanking the Lord.*" These words suggest that the instrumentalists and singers joined in unison.

In turning now to the Psalms themselves, we have a few indications in the titles of some of these. In fifty-five Psalms a note in the title says that the psalm is "For the chief musician;" some guide as to the meaning of this may be gathered from 1 Chronicles xxiii. 4, where the verbal form of this word (*lamnazêach*) occurs, and means "to preside over," and from 1 Chronicles xv. 21, where it means "to lead," in reference to instrumental accompaniment. What the direction contained in this title meant, therefore, probably was that the psalm in question had been written for the "leader" of the singers; the reference being, of course, to the Temple singers. This title, in fact, implied that the psalms to which it was prefixed were composed specially for use in the public worship of the Temple. This does not mean that psalms *not* bearing this title were not intended

[1] See further Exod. xv. 20; 1 Sam. xviii. 6; and important are 1 Sam. x. 5; xix. 20.

for public worship; but it gives a definite character to those which have it, and stamps them as belonging to a specific category. It is also very probable that some psalms, which originally were without this title, received it in later times when they were adapted to use in the worship of the Temple.

Three psalms have the title, "Upon" or "According to Gittith" (R.V. "set to Gittith"). It is possible that this refers to a particular kind of instrument, to the accompaniment of which the Psalms in question were sung. This is implied in the Targum to the Psalms, where it is said that "Gittith" referred to an instrument that came from Gath; the grammatical form of the word would support this. A more probable explanation, however, is that "set to Gittith" refers to the tune of a vintage song; for in the Midrash on the Psalms, it is said to refer to the words in Joel iii. 13: "*Put ye in the sickle, for the vintage is ripe; come, tread ye, for the wine-press* (the Hebrew word is *gath*) *is full, the fats overflow.*" It is quite possible that these words are from some popular vintage song,[1] the melody of which was well known, and that the psalmist intended the psalms in question to be sung to this tune.[2]

We get a more definite indication as to the kind of

[1] The adaptation by the prophet of a quotation from such a song, utilising it for the purpose of pronouncing a doom, would have brought home his message with all the greater force to the hearts of his hearers.

[2] See what is said on p. 74.

musical accompaniment in the case of the titles to Psalms iv., vi., liv., lv., lxvii., lxxvi.: "With stringed instruments" *(Binĕgînoth)*; this means that the singing of these psalms was to be accompanied by stringed instruments, *i.e.* harps (see 1 Chronicles xv. 21). In the same way Psalm v. was to be sung, according to the direction in the title, to the accompaniment of flutes or pipes (see Isaiah xxx. 29). Again, in the title to Psalm xlvi., it is directed that the psalm is to be sung "Upon Alâmôth;"[1] this, in all probability, refers to instruments with strings of a high pitch; the expression occurs also in 1 Chronicles xv. 20, in connexion with stringed instruments. Once more, in the titles to Psalms vi. and xii., the direction given is that they are to be accompanied "on the octave" (*Al-hashsheminith*), *i.e.*, an eight-stringed instrument tuned an octave lower than the voices.[2]

Apart from the titles we have in the Psalms themselves some further *data* as to the part played by the musical accompaniment. First, as to two difficult terms the meaning of which can be only tentatively put forth. In Psalm ix. 16 occurs the word *higgaion*, as a musical direction; and it means there, probably, that the musical accompaniment is to burst forth with a deep, solemn sound. The word occurs elsewhere in the Psalter, though not as a musical expression, but in

[1] *Lit.* "After the manner of maidens," *i.e.*, in reference to high-pitched voices; see further on this, p. 116.

[2] *Cp.* Midrash *Tehillim* on these two psalms.

the text; thus in Psalm xcii. 3 the Psalmist says he will praise God "with a solemn sound"; in Isaiah xxxi. 4 a word from the same root is used of the deep growling of a lion, in Isaiah xxxviii. 14 of the low cooing of a dove, and in Isaiah xvi. 7 of the moaning of those in grief. This use of the root seems to imply that as a musical direction it meant that the accompaniment of the instruments was, at the point indicated, to be of a low, solemn character; this would, in the one place in the Psalms where it occurs, be peculiarly appropriate, for the words of the passage are: *The Lord hath made Himself known, He hath executed judgement, the wicked is snared in the work of his own hands*; *i.e.* the pronouncement of doom. The other expression is *Selah*; this occurs seventy-one times in the Psalter, but never in a title, always in the body of the psalm, and practically always at the end of a strophe or a division. "Its reference to the Temple music is evinced by the fact that thirty-one of the thirty-nine Psalms containing it are ascribed in their titles 'for the chief musician.'"[1] The meaning of the word has been much disputed, so that here again one cannot speak with certainty; some scholars regard it as derived from a root meaning "to lift up"; in this case, the direction being to the instrumental accompaniment, it must have meant that the instruments were to play loudly. There is, however, good reason for the view that it meant a break in the music (see *Oxford Hebrew*

[1] Hastings D.B. iv. 431b.

Lexicon, s. v.). It is used in the *Shemoneh Esreh* after the Third and Eighteenth Benedictions, and in other early Jewish prayers, showing knowledge of its use in practice about 100 A.D. St. Jerome classes *Selah* with *Amen* and *Shalom*, "Peace." "It probably came into use in the late Persian period in connexion with psalms used with musical accompaniment in public worship, to indicate the place of Benedictions."[1]

Next, we must turn to the actual text of some of the Psalms, as here, too, we are enabled to gain some information regarding the musical accompaniment to the singing.

Psalm xxxiii. 2, 3: "Give thanks unto the Lord with harp (*kinnor*), sing praises unto Him with the psaltery (*nebel*) of ten strings. Sing unto Him a new song, play skilfully with a loud noise" (*lit.*, play skilfully on stringed instruments with a shout).

The Hebrew word for "Give thanks" is the regular one used for ritual worship, and is perhaps better rendered by "Praise," *cp.* Psalm xxviii. 7: "With my song will I praise Him." The words "with the harp" illustrate the way in which the singer accompanied his song, *cp.* Psalm lvii. 8. "Sing unto Him a new song" means, according to Briggs,[2] a fresh outburst of song; the expression occurs several times in the Psalms (xl. 4, xcvi. 1., xcviii. 1., cxliv. 9, cxlix. 1). "Play skilfully" refers to the accompaniment of the

[1] *Ibid.* This would point, therefore, to a break in the music.
[2] *Op. cit.* i. p. 292.

harp, in Hebrew the word is *naggên*, the regular word for playing on a stringed instrument. "With a shout" is either to be taken literally as the sacred shout (1 Sam. iv. 5, 6, Psalms xxvii. 6, Job viii. 21, xxxiii. 26), or else it may refer to the trumpet-sound, as in Psalm xlvii. 5.

Psalm xliii. 4: "Upon the harp (*kinnor*) will I praise thee, O God, my God." As it was only the Levites who in the Temple praised God with the accompaniment of the harp, this verse shows that the Psalm was composed by one of the Temple musicians.

Psalm lxviii. 24, 25. "They have seen thy goings, O God, even the goings of my God, my King, into the sanctuary. The singers went before, the minstrels followed after, in the midst of the damsels playing with timbrels."

This does not refer to worship, but to a procession formed in order to go up to the Temple to worship; the mention here, therefore, of damsels is no proof that these took part in the actual Temple worship.[1] The verse describes the ascent of the Temple musicians on their way to the sanctuary; the damsels accompany them, but do not form part of the procession. The Revised Version makes the meaning of the Hebrew clear, "in the midst of the damsels." As a rule, the singers accompanied their song themselves; in this passage the singers and instrumentalists are differentiated. The Hebrew word for "minstrels" is

[1] See further on this, p. 116; and *cp.* Exod. xv. 20.

"players on stringed instruments." We learn from this passage that the stringed instruments were, therefore, not too large to carry in procession (*cp.* 2 Chron. xx. 28).

Psalm lxxi. 22: "I will praise thee with the psaltery," *lit.* "with the instrument of the harp." This is the only place in the Psalms where this expression occurs, though once elsewhere in the Bible it is used (1 Chron. xvi. 5) in the plural. That it was played only as an accompaniment is seen from the words which follow: "My lips shall greatly rejoice when I sing praise unto Thee."

Psalm lxxxi. 1-3: "Sing aloud unto God our strength; make a joyful noise unto the God of Jacob. Take up the psalm, and bring hither (better "strike") the timbrel, the pleasant harp with the psaltery. Blow up the trumpet in the new moon."

This is an instructive passage, for it describes the singing of the psalm as being accompanied by an instrument of percussion (timbrel=*tôph*), by stringed instruments (harp=*nebel*, psaltery=*kinnor*) and by a wind instrument (trumpet=*shôphar*, properly ram's-horn). The harp and psaltery would perhaps be better rendered by "harp and lyre"; the two are often mentioned together (*e.g.* Psalms xcii. 3, cviii. 2, cl. 3), the difference between them being probably in the number of the strings (see below). In Psalm xxx. 2, the *nebel*—*i.e.* harp in the more usual sense—is spoken of as having ten strings; in connexion with this it is well to remember what has been said in an earlier chapter, that among Orientals the intervals from note to note are smaller than a semitone, so that a ten-stringed harp would not necessarily have a compass of more than from three to four tones. It was evidently a larger instrument than the lyre (*kinnor*) which, according to St. Jerome (*Comm. in Psalm* xxx. 2) had six strings. The trumpet (*shôphar*) was originally a ram's-horn, and therefore curved in shape; later on it was made of metal, and straightened, as can be seen from the bas-relief on the arch of Titus. The ram's-horn is still used on certain occasions in the Synagogue.

Psalms xcii. 1-3: "It is a good thing to give thanks unto the Lord . . . With an instrument of ten strings and with the psaltery; with a solemn sound upon the harp."

The words, "with an instrument of ten strings and with the psaltery" do not refer to two different instruments; they might equally well be rendered, "with an instrument of ten strings, yea with the psaltery (*nebel*)." The Septuagint reads "a ten-stringed nebel." In Hebrew, "a solemn sound" is "higgaion" [on this, see p. 56]; this word used in connexion with harp (better "lyre" = *kinnor*) suggests that the *kinnor* was a lower-pitched instrument than the *nebel.*

Lastly, in Psalm cl. 3-5, we have apparently an enumeration of all the musical instruments used in Temple worship to accompany the singing of psalms;

trumpet (*shôphar*), psaltery (*nebel*), harp (*kinnor*), timbrel (*tôph*), stringed instruments (*minim*), pipe (*ugab*), cymbals (*zelzelim*). Reference has been to all of these above, with the exception of *minim*, a word which occurs here only (perhaps also in xlv. 9, according to the emendation suggested by some scholars); it is a loan-word from the Aramaic, and is a general term for "strings" (cp. *Oxford Hebrew Lexicon*, s.v.), and refers to the stringed instruments mentioned in the context.

CHAPTER IV.

THE ANTECEDENTS OF THE PSALMS.

THE earliest Hebrew words for "song" are *shîr* and *shîrah;* in their origin neither necessarily connoted anything sacred.[1] The most developed stage in the history of song among the Israelites is represented by the Psalms. But development implies an antecedent of some kind; there must, therefore, have been some form, or forms, of song which preceded that with which we are now familiar in the Psalter. Further, even a superficial glance at the Psalms shows that they vary greatly in subject-matter and character; this variation is so pronounced that one is justified, as we shall try and show, in regarding different Psalms as the representatives of different *types* of song. The Psalms representing these various types must, then, be regarded as the same in kind, though differing from them in form, as earlier songs belonging to the same types respectively. Is it possible to indicate the nature of the earlier songs belonging to the several types? The object of this

[1] See *e.g.*, Gen. xxxi. 27.

chapter is to try and show that there is some justification for answering this question in the affirmative. We shall be guided in this partly by analogy, partly by the nature of things, and partly by the contents of some of the Psalms.

But it must be added, and stress is laid on the fact, that not *all* the psalms necessarily represent developed forms of particular types. Circumstances may arise under the influence of which wholly new types are called into existence; and that such circumstances did arise during the history of Israel, and became the means of originating some entirely new types of psalm, can be proved. Attention will be called to these later on. For the moment we are concerned with types of which, it is contended, representatives existed before the Psalms, as we now have them, took their present shape.

§ I. *Songs*[1] *in honour of the Deity; and songs which commemorate the heroic deeds of ancestors.*

Although these two types came in later times to be wholly differentiated, in their earlier forms this was not the case; an instance will be given presently. Two subjects which all peoples, when they have reached a certain stage of culture, love to commemorate and to dwell upon in song are the wondrous acts of their gods and the heroic deeds of their ancestors in days gone by.

[1] We use the word "song" because it best represents the Hebrew *shîr*; but it will be understood that it is used in the widest sense.

"We have in epic poetry and legend the romantic and heroic tales of the great civilized races, or races which have proved capable of civilization. These are the Indians, the Greeks, Romans, Celts, Scandinavians, and Germans. These have won their way into the national literatures and the region of epic. We find them in the *Odyssey*, the *Edda*, the Celtic poems, the *Ramazana*, and they even appear in the *Veda*. They occur in the legends and pedigrees of the royal heroes of Greece and Germany. . . . The characters are national heroes, such as Perseus, Jason, Œdipus, and Olympian gods."[1] The forms in which these traditions now exist, viz. in the *Odyssey*, etc., are highly developed ones, and they must have existed in substance for a long period of time before they assumed the form in which we know them now. But these traditions are not confined to the peoples enumerated, to them might well have been added the Egyptians,[2] Babylonians,[3] and Israelites, who also have their poetry and legend containing romantic and heroic tales, though, in the case of the two former, they have not come down to us in the same developed form as in the case of the other peoples mentioned; while, as regards the Israelites, the form is for the most part so spiritualized that it is only here

[1] Andrew Lang, *Myth, Ritual, and Religion*, ii. p. 304 (The Silver Library). *Cp.* further Gunkel, *Genesis*, Einleitung, § i-iv. (1901).

[2] See *e.g.* Andrew Lang, *Op. cit.* ii. pp. 106 ff.

[3] See *e.g.*, C. J. Ball, *Light from the East*, pp. 1 ff., 34 ff. (1899); J. G. Frazer, *The Golden Bough*, iii. pp. 160 ff. (1900).

and there in their songs that one is able to discern signs of the early traditions.

Tacitus, in his *De Situ, Moribus et Populis Germaniae* (chap. ii.), tells us concerning the Germani, that "in their ancient songs—for it is among them the only method whereby they remember things and record their past history—they celebrate Tuisco, an earth-born god, and his son Mannus, as the originators and founders of their race;"[1] and, in the next chapter, in speaking of their war-songs, he says that they tell of how once Hercules sojourned in their midst, and that when they go into battle they sing of this man, the greatest of all heroes.[2] Many other examples of this kind of thing could be given; all ancient races preserved legends of their gods and records of the heroic deeds of their ancestors in the national songs;[3] and, according to the earliest traditions, the greatest national heroes were gods, or at all events descended from gods. That this was a very natural proceeding among the races of antiquity will be obvious to anyone who considers the matter; there is, therefore, no need to labour the point. The analogy of the custom among many races is presumptive evidence of the existence of a like custom among the ancient Israelites

[1] Celebrant carminibus antiquis—quod unum apud illos memoriae et annalium genus est—Tuistionem deum terra editum, et filium Mannum, originem gentis conditoresque.

[2] Fuisse apud eos et Herculē memorant, primumque omnium virorum fortium. Ituri in prœlia canunt.

[3] *Cp. e.g.*, Andrew Lang's *Custom and Myth*, passim.

and their ancestors; but we have in the Old Testament more tangible proof than this, to which reference will be made presently. It must be remembered, let it be said in passing, that topics such as those just referred to would clearly have occupied the minds of men in the nomadic stage far more than when settled life brought with it agricultural pursuits and the like, and therefore the songs in which they were commemorated would represent a type which must be regarded as the most ancient. It is, of course, not to be expected that in the Old Testament any of the songs in vogue during the nomadic stage of Israel's ancestors have been preserved; the development of religious belief would preclude the possibility of this, apart from other reasons; but echoes of the *type* of song we are considering are certainly to be found there. For example, Judges v. is, as regards subject-matter, exactly the kind of song which, in much simpler forms, had been sung from time immemorial. Later generations always adapt traditional modes to changing circumstances, but the various *types* are the same; and in Judges v. we have the representative of a particular type. This song has a special interest because it exhibits what later on became two different types of ancient song. On the analogy of the custom among other races the assumption may be made that in the earliest form of this type among the ancestors of the Israelites, the race's gods, and the national heroes, were not differentiated. With a deeper knowledge of

Jehovah came the realisation of an infinite difference between God and men, and the songs which had as their subject the mighty deeds of Jehovah in ancient days became a different type from those which commemorated the heroic deeds of ancestors. Now, Judges v. seems to reflect a transitional stage in the history of this type of song among the Israelites; for, while differentiating between the "leaders of Israel" and Jehovah, both are commemorated as warriors in this song. It must surely be an antique conception of Jehovah which is expressed in these words:

> "Lord, when Thou wentest forth out of Seir,
> When Thou marchedst out of the field of Edom,
> The earth trembled, the heavens also dropped,
> Yea, the clouds dropped water" (verse 4).

Or again:

> "The Lord came down for me against (or "among")
> the mighty" (verse 13).

And once more:

> "Curse ye, Meroz, said the angel of the Lord . . .
> Because they came not to the help of the Lord,
> To the help of the Lord against (or "among")
> the mighty" (verse 23).

It must be remembered that even in much later times it was believed that supernatural beings came to the help of Israel in battle (see 2 Samuel v. 23-25, 2 Macc. iii. 24-26, x. 29, 30).[1] In Judges v., then, the leaders of Israel, and Jehovah, are both celebrated for championing the cause of Israel in battle; but they are differentiated; that is a modification of the earlier form of this type of song. Later on, as we shall see, some songs told of the mighty acts of Jehovah in ancient days, while others commemorated the heroic deeds of the nation's ancestors; and thus, two entirely different types of song arose.

What may be regarded as a further indication of the existence of songs which told of the mighty acts of Israel's God is the reference in 1 Samuel v. 8; here we have the account of how the Israelites brought the ark of God into the battle against the Philistines, and these latter say: "God is come into the camp; woe unto us! for there hath not been such a thing heretofore. Woe unto us! these are the gods that smote the Egyptians with all manner of plagues in the wilderness." It is the last sentence here which is important in the present connexion, for it points to the existence of a popular traditional account of the mighty acts of the national God of Israel; if such existed—and it is hardly possible to doubt that this was so—it is certain to have been set in rhythmical form. The way in which the subject is brought in in the passage before us implies that what is referred to was well-known, and

[1] How widespread this belief was may be seen by consulting Dr. J. Rendel Harris' *The Cult of the Heavenly Twins*, passim (1906).

for things of this kind to be well-known meant, in the case of ancient peoples, that they were commemorated in song. Things of national concern, like the deliverance from Egypt, tend to assume a stereotyped form; they are also more easily recited and more easily remembered when this form is rhythmical; besides which, the fact of their dealing with a subject which was sacred, *i.e.*, the interposition of Jehovah, necessitated, according to a general custom among ancient peoples, something in the shape of poetical structure which was recited according to a set mode. When we read, therefore, in Exodus xiii. 8: "And thou shalt tell it thy son in that day, saying, It is because of that which the Lord did for me when I came forth out of Egypt," we may feel tolerably certain that this handing-down from father to son of the account of the mighty acts of Jehovah was recited from generation to generation in the form of song, though the form was undoubtedly very simple, and the "melody" little more than a modulated monotone.

We conclude, therefore, that among the antecedents of the Psalms there were, firstly, two types: that in which the mighty acts of Jehovah were celebrated, and that in which the heroic deeds of the nation's ancestors were commemorated.

§ II. *Songs which preserved the memory of great national events.*

It is not to be expected that one type of song

can always be kept wholly differentiated from all other types; in the main, no doubt, special features are seen to be characteristic of a particular type, but from the nature of the case it happens sometimes that in certain respects two types become related. One of the two types of song referred to in the preceding section, namely, that which commemorated the heroic deeds of ancestors—and to some extent the other as well—must in time have given rise to another type, which one may call the *historical ode*, *i.e.*, a song which preserved the memory of some great national event. A song of this kind, which represents a distinct type, will, however, be sometimes associated with the God of Israel, sometimes with one of the nation's heroes, and, in so far, partakes of the characteristic feature of some one or other type; that is inevitable, because great national events are usually associated with some outstanding character, or else, especially among the Israelites, with the national God. Nevertheless, the historical ode, which deals with some particular event, is in its essence different from the two types already referred to, and may therefore be regarded as a distinct type, though lineally descended from these. Then, again, the historical ode will, according to its tenor, be either a song of victory or a lament; for example, the song in Numbers xxi. 27-30, "Come ye to Heshbon," is a song of victory; while David's lament over Saul and Jonathan (2 Samuel i. 19-27) is a dirge; each preserves the memory of a national event. So that the historical ode must be sub-divided into two classes : the song of triumph, and the dirge.

§ III. *Folk-Songs.*

In Num. xxi. 17, 18, occurs the so-called "Song of the Well":

> "Spring up, O well; sing ye unto it;
> To the well which the princes digged,
> Which the nobles of the people delved,
> With the wand, and with their staves."

This song belongs to the class of what one may call the early popular poetry of the Israelites. "Such poetry consisted especially of short snatches sung in honour of the vine at time of vintage, or of wells and springs, and even, as Ewald put it, 'of popular songs accompanying the alternate strokes of hard labour.' No complete vintage song survives, though a line of one is probably quoted in Is. lxv. 8. [*cp.* Ps. lvii. title, see below], and imitations of the class may be found in Is. v. 1 ff., xxvii. 2-5. The present lines are a complete, or all but complete, popular song, addressed to a well, in which, perhaps, as W. R. Smith suggested, 'the Hebrew women, as they stand round the fountain waiting their turn to draw, coax forth the water, which wells up all too slowly for their impatience.' Budde may be right in detecting in the song an allusion to a custom, by which when a well had been discovered it was lightly covered over, and then, on a subsequent occasion, solemnly opened with a symbolic action of the sceptre-like staves of the Sheikhs of the clan, and formally declared clan property. Two interesting parallels are cited; Kazwini (i. 189) relates: 'When the water [of the wells of Ilabistan] failed, a feast was held at the source, with music and dancing, to induce it to flow again.' And Nilus (Migne, *Patrologia Græca*, tom lxxix. col. 648), as Goldziher (*Abhandlungen*, i. 58) has pointed out, reports of the nomadic Arabs, that when they found a well they danced by it and sang songs to it. Modern travellers speak of the songs used by the Bedawin as they draw water for their flocks (Seetzen, *Reisen*, ii. 223)."[1]

These indications all point to the fact of the existence of early popular poetry among the Israelites. A poem of this class was usually of a joyous character, into which, generally speaking, a certain religious element entered; and such poem or song was called a *shîr*. Robertson Smith traces a distinct connexion between an example of this type of song, and one of the Psalms: "A curious and interesting feature in the musical titles in the earlier half of the Psalter is that many of them indicate the tune to which the Psalm was set, by quoting phrases like *Aijeleth*[*hash-*] *shahar*, or *Jonath elem rechokim*, which are evidently the names of familiar songs. Similarly the ancient Syrian

[1] Buchanan Gray, *Numbers*, pp. 288 f. (International Critical Commentary.)

hymn-writers prefix to the compositions such musical titles as 'To the tune of *I will open my mouth with knowledge.*' Of the song which gave the title *Al-taschith,*[1] 'Destroy not,' a trace is still preserved in Is. lxv. 8: 'When the new wine is found in the cluster,' says the prophet, 'men say, *Destroy it not for a blessing is in it.*' These words in the Hebrew have a distinct lyric rhythm. They are the first line of one of the vintage songs so often alluded to in Scripture. And so we learn that the early religious melody of Israel had a popular origin, and was closely connected with the old joyous life of the nation.'"[2] Regarding the other title mentioned here by Robertson Smith, *Jonath elem rechokim* ("The silent dove of them that are far away"), which is evidently the title of some ancient popular song, we may perhaps discern a reference to it in Ps. lv. 67: "O that I had wings like a dove, then would I fly away and be at rest; lo, then would I wander far off; I would lodge in the wilderness." Briggs, in referring to titles like those cited, says: "It is hardly possible that the reference could have been to a melody. It was doubtless to a tone for cantillation, as the tones of the early Synagogue and early Church, which are capable of use in pieces of different measure and different strophical length."[3] This does not, however, necessarily controvert Robertson Smith's contention,

[1] Pss. lvii. lix., lxxv.
[2] *The Old Testament in the Jewish Church*, p. 209.
[3] *The Book of Psalms*, p. lxxv. (International Critical Commentary).

for by the word "melody," one does not, when speaking of ancient times, understand it to mean anything like the modern idea of a tune; nevertheless, it is worth remembering that some early forms of tune contain the elements of what even in modern times may be regarded as quite passable.[1]

Another type, therefore, of ancient song in Israel was the folk-song, under which we include harvest and vintage songs. Folk-songs in the ordinary sense of the word, cannot, strictly speaking, be spoken of as among the antecedents of the Psalms, though even here it is well not to speak dogmatically; but in the case of harvest and vintage songs it is different, and we shall try and show in the next chapter that certain psalms, or at any rate, parts of certain psalms, may quite possibly contain, in a developed form, echoes of this type of song.

§ IV.—Finally, one other type of song was that which expressed a prayer, or hope, or, perhaps chiefly, a *meditation.* This would certainly have been one of the latest types of all, but that something of the kind must have come into existence at a comparatively early date, can scarcely be doubted when it is remembered how abundantly the religious instinct found expression among the Israelites of all ages. An example of this type is the Song of Hannah (though this is evidently a somewhat developed form of song).

Of the various types of "song" mentioned, all,

[1] See above, Chap. I.

excepting the last, were intended for public use; but even in the case of this, it would be precarious to assert that it was necessarily restricted to private use. David's *Lament* was, as we know, meant for public recitation (see 2 Sam. i. 18) in spite of its being individual in form.

It is certain that none of these various types of song were written down when first uttered, though their developed counterparts in later days were probably, at any rate in many instances, very soon committed to writing. "The old poets did not write their poems. Each of them had his *rawi*, or 'reciter,' who learned each poem, and transmitted it to others."[1]

The types of "song" which (with the exception perhaps, of the last) we have assumed to have been in existence in some form or another, long before the time of the monarchy, and which may therefore be regarded as the antecedents of the Psalms, are the following:—

(i.) Legends, or the like, concerning the mighty deeds of Jehovah in primeval days; these developed later into songs of praise.

(ii.) Songs commemorating the heroic deeds of ancestors; these developed later into the historical ode, of which two kinds existed: the song of triumph and the dirge.

(iii.) Harvest and Vintage songs.

(iv.) Meditations, issuing later into the "Individual" psalms proper.

[1] *Encycl. Bibl.* 3943.

There may, probably enough, have been other types as well, but we are only concerned with those which may reasonably be regarded as antecedents of similar types to be found among the Psalms.

Our next task must be to try and show by means of definite examples that there are grounds for believing that many of the psalms, as we now have them, are developed forms of types which were in existence long before the earliest psalms in the Psalter were composed.

CHAPTER V.

THE CONSTITUENT ELEMENTS OF THE PSALTER.

BEFORE seeking to substantiate what has been said in the preceding chapter it is essential to realise how composite, both in structure and authorship, the contents of the Psalter are. Its composite character is seen not only in the fact that it embodies collections of songs belonging to different ages and to different authors; but, what is still more important from our present point of view, that individual psalms are also composite.

§ I. *The composite character of the Psalms.*

There is abundant evidence in the Psalter itself, as will be seen presently, to show its composite character; but it may be well, first, to draw attention to one or two authoritative *dicta* in Jewish writings; what is said in these would not be accepted nowadays as witnessing to the actual facts of the case, but they prove that in the Jewish Church itself the composite character of the Psalter was recognised as an indubitable fact. We find, for example, a difference of opinion as to how many psalms the Psalter in its present form contains; thus, it is said at least twice that there are only a hundred and forty-seven psalms, so in the Babylonian Talmud *Sopherim* xvi. 11: "The 147 songs which are written in the book of the Psalms are according to the years of Jacob" (see Genesis xlvii. 28); the same is said in *Berakhoth* 9*b* 10*a*; this number was gained because Psalms i. and ii., xlii. and xliii., lxxi. and lxxii., were respectively reckoned as one psalm. On the other hand, a hundred and fifty is stated to be the number in *Kiddushin* 30*a*.[1] The psalms without a title, thirty-five in all, are not ascribed to David, but are simply called the "Orphan Psalms" (*Abodah Zara* 24*b*). Then again, it is recognised that the Psalms have been edited; not of course in the sense in which we should use the word in reference to the Psalter now; but, at any rate, it was realised that the form in which we now have the Psalms was not the original one; thus in the Talmud, according to Hamburger (though the reference is not given), Samuel both collected and edited the Psalms.[2] A different tradition is contained in a *Baraitha*[3] of the Talmudic tractrate *Baba Bathra* (quoted by Briggs, *Op. cit.* I. p. 54):

[1] In the Greek Bible there are 151 psalms. See further, on the numbering of the Psalms, Briggs, *Op. cit.* I. p. lxxxviii.

[2] Possibly a reference is intended to Psalm xcix. 6.

[3] The *Baraithas* are ancient traditions not incorporated in the *Mishna*.

"David wrote the Book of Psalms with the aid of ten ancients, with the aid of Adam the first, Melchizedek, Abraham, Moses, Heman, Jeduthun, Asaph, and the three sons of Korah"; as Briggs says: "The writing of David here is evidently editorship . . . . the statement comes from the second century A.D., and is stereotyped in Jewish tradition." The titles to many of the Psalms witness, further, to the belief in the Jewish Church that the Psalter was of composite authorship; only seventy-four are ascribed to David, twelve are ascribed to Asaph, eleven to the sons of Korah, one each to Moses, Solomon, Heman, Ethan, and 'Oni ("the afflicted one"), while forty-eight are anonymous.

It is, however, more important for our present purpose to show that many of the individual psalms are composite in structure and authorship; they have not, in many cases, come down to us in their original form; additions have sometimes been made for liturgical purposes; some psalms, originally forming one whole, have been divided into two; in the case of some of the earliest psalms it is highly probable that they have undergone revision in order to adapt them to the religious thought of later times. We can only give a few examples (the subject is exhaustively dealt with in commentaries on the Psalms),[1] as our object is merely to try

[1] *E.g.* those of Ewald, Baethgen, Duhm, Cheyne, Kirkpatrick, Briggs.

and show that many of the psalms have a history behind them.

A striking instance of the mutilation of a psalm is seen in Psalms ix., x.; that these in an earlier stage formed one is proved by the fact that each is an acrostic of *half* the alphabet[1]; Psalm ix. goes to "K," Psalm x. commences at "L"; the object of dividing the original psalm in this way is difficult to determine[2]; but in view of the distinct difference both in tone and subject between the two halves, it is possible that the amalgamation as given in the *Septuagint* and in the *Vulgate* represents a second stage in the literary structure of the two psalms, and that the Hebrew form reflects the earliest stage; that an editor, say of the early post-exilic period, should take a delight in moulding two originally distinct psalms into one acrostic whole is quite comprehensible—both the psalms in question bear considerable marks of text manipulation—the desire to produce a literary curiosity, as regards structure,[3] sufficiently explains the object of this. Such a proceeding would only offer an interesting example, in addition to many others, of the freedom with which the early scribes adapted their literary possessions

In the Septuagint and in the Vulgate the two form only one psalm.

[2] Kirkpatrick (*in loc.*) says; "The two psalms present an unsolved literary problem . . . . Ps. ix., however, appears to be complete in itself, and it seems preferable to regard Ps. x. as a companion piece rather than a part of a continuous whole."

[3] *Cp.* other acrostic Psalms, such as xxv., cxix., etc.

to changing circumstances. Again, that Psalms xlii. and xliii. were originally one needs no proof, one has but to read them to become convinced of the fact; the two "form a connected poem, consisting of three equal stanzas, each ending with the same refrain. The same circumstances appear to lie in the background, and the tone, spirit, and language are the same throughout. The prayer of Psalm xliii. is needed to supplement the complaint of Psalm xlii."[1] The separation of what was originally one psalm was due in all probability, as Dean Kirkpatrick points out, to liturgical reasons. It is evidently also due to the same cause that we have a number of instances of the inverse process, namely those in which different psalms have been combined into one; these are enumerated by Briggs[2]; to give but two examples out of about twenty-five: Psalm cviii. is composed of vv. 1-6 (= lvii. 8-12) and vv. 7-14 (= lx. 7-14); not that the redactor of this Psalm necessarily used parts of lvii. and lx., but that he used some antecedent form of them.

Again, on comparing Ps. xl. 13-17 with Ps. lxx. one sees at once that the former is really an edited form of the latter appended to xl. 1-12. The following should also be compared, xxxi. 1-13 with lxxi. 1-3, cxv. 4-18 with cxxxiv. 15-21. These are all very obvious cases of the process of adding pieces of one

[1] Kirkpatrick *in loc.* [2] *Op. cit.* I. pp. xlix. ff.

psalm on to another; and this, again, illustrates the truth that many of the psalms have, for one reason or another, been altered and adapted. But there are many other instances of this kind of thing having taken place, and a careful study of the Psalms leads to the conviction that Briggs is right when, in speaking of the various kinds of glosses found in them, he says: "The simplest and most natural are liturgical in character, petitions, intercessions, calls to worship, expressions of praise, and the like. Psalms expressive of piety and protestations of integrity are modified by the insertions of confessions of sin and pleas for forgiveness. Protestations of innocence are inserted in psalms which lament the sufferings of the people of God from vindictive and cruel enemies. Personal, local, and earlier national relations are generalised so that earlier psalms might with propriety be used in the public worship of later times. Early psalms were adapted to the time of the supremacy of Law by legal glosses, to the times of Hebrew Wisdom by legal glosses, to the Maccabæan times by lamentations for defeat, imprecations upon enemies, and other warlike expressions appropriate to a period of persecution and conflict. Early psalms were enriched by illustrations from earlier literature, or by fuller and expansive statements. Several psalms were given a Messianic reference in this way. Thus the editors of the various Psalters did exactly what the editors of prayer-books, liturgies and hymn-books have always done. They had greater interest in editing the psalms for public worship than in preserving their original literary form and meaning. Accordingly, many of the psalms have lost their original literary form. They express varied states of mind, differences of experience, inconsistent situations; there are sudden and unexpected changes in tenses of verbs, and in person and number of pronouns and suffixes. All this makes the Psalms richer in the expression of religious experience, and in this respect more suited to the varied needs of the congregation, but greatly injures their literary and historic value."[1]

There is thus every justification for the belief that many of the psalms as we now have them have gone through a process of evolution, and this not only in structure, but also in content. This is a considerable step towards establishing the further contention that many of the psalms as they now appear are developed forms of types which were in existence long before the earliest psalms in the Psalter were composed.

§ II. *Some examples of developed forms of earlier types of song.*

In the preceding chapter it was suggested that the antecedents of the Psalms comprised at least four different types of song whose developed counterparts

[1] *Op. cit.* I. p. l.

were to be discerned in the Psalter; to try and substantiate this is our present task. The attempt is worth making, for among many critics of to-day there is a tendency to regard the whole Book of the Psalms as a, comparatively speaking, late literary production; we are far from denying that a large number of the psalms were originally composed in post-exilic times, some belonging to as late a time as the Maccabæan period; but to maintain that not one, or scarcely one, of the Psalms is pre-exilic, as some writers have done, is difficult to believe; for it must be remembered, on the one hand, that among the Israelites, as among other ancient peoples, the earliest form of literary production was the poetic; and, on the other hand, that the Israelites were essentially a musical and poetical people, and the national genius which produced the admittedly late Psalms is unlikely to have been inactive in earlier times. All critics are agreed that we have, outside the Psalter, some really ancient poetical pieces in the Old Testament,[1] which witness to the existence of the national poetical genius; but if it be said that practically none of the Psalms belong to pre-exilic times, this seems to create a strange hiatus in the history of song among the Israelites which is not easy to account for. Our contention is that in substance, though not in form, a considerable

[1] Such as Gen. iv. 23, 24, Num. xxi. 14, 15, xxi. 17, 18, Judg. v. 2-31.

proportion of the Psalms belong to pre-exilic times. The preceding chapters have, it is hoped, suggested the probability of this. We proceed now to try and show that the study of certain psalms bears out this contention.

(*a*) The first type of song regarded, in the last chapter, as being antecedent to some of the psalms was that which spoke of the mighty deeds of the national God in primeval days. An example of this is the fragment of an ancient ode which is one of two elements (see further under (*c*)) incorporated into Ps. lxv.; verses 6, 7 (7, 8 in Hebr.) run literally:

> "Who arrangeth the mountains by His strength,
> Girded with might;
> Who stilleth the raging of the seas,
> The roaring of their waves."

The reference here is to the Creation and to Jehovah's conflict with Tehom, the primeval watery monster. A distinct community of ideas seems to exist between this passage and Jer. x. 12, 13: "He hath made the earth by his power, he hath established the world by his wisdom, and by his understanding hath he stretched out the heavens [the words which follow, "when he uttereth his voice," are omitted by the *Septuagint*]; there is a tumult of the waters in the heavens. . . ." These identical words occur again in Is. li. 15, 16, a fact which strengthens the supposition that they represent part of a well-known ancient song; possibly Ps. lxv. 6, 7, belongs to the same song from which the Jeremiah passage has been taken. In each case, at any rate, it is the distant past to which reference is made; and this act of Jehovah's must have been commemorated in song from very ancient times;[1] part of this song was utilized to proclaim the might of the God of Israel in the psalm of praise which we now have in Ps. lxv. That the subject of this ancient song should have been handled by David in a hymn of praise would have been a very natural thing, so that it is quite possible that, in this case at all events, the Davidic ascription in the title may rest on sound tradition. The subject of this fragment is more elaborately dealt with in Ps. lxxiv.; here we have in verses 12-15 the following extract from (or, at any rate, reminiscence of) this ancient song:

"God is my king from of old,
Working salvation in the midst of the earth;
Thou didst split in twain the Sea in thy strength,
Thou didst break in pieces the heads of the dragons in the waters;
Thou didst shatter the heads of Leviathan;
Thou wilt give him for food,—for food to the denizens of the waste;
Thou didst cleave fountain and flood;
Thou didst dry up ancient rivers."

The same notes which are sounded in the previous

[1] See, further, the writer's *The Evolution of the Messianic Idea*, pp. 60 ff.

passage recur here, only in more detail; the reference is to something which happened long ago; the God of Israel overcame a great monster, who is the Sea personified, and who is also called Leviathan. The occurrence is clearly regarded as well known, and must have been the subject of song for ages before it appeared in its present form. It is also worth noticing that in the verses which follow (16, 17) there is a reference to the Creation; the same is the case in the context of the former passage cited; it is very probable that the great creative acts of Jehovah were also the subject of song long before they appeared in some of our psalms in their present form.

Again, in Ps. lxxxix., 8-10 (9-11 in Hebr.), the primeval conflict of Jehovah is the subject of song:

> "Jehovah, God of hosts, who is like unto Thee, Mighty Jah?
> And thy faithfulness is round about thee.
> Thou hast the pre-eminence over the Sea when she ariseth,
> Thou stillest her waves when they roar (*cp.* the *Septuagint*),
> Thou didst humble (*cp.* the *Septuagint*) Rahab, as one that is dishonoured (*cp.* Ezek. xxi. 30);
> With thy mighty arm (*cp.* verse 13 of this Ps.) hast thou scattered thine enemies."

Again it is something which happened in the distant past which is sung of here, a glorious act on the part of Israel's national God; it is also again brought in incidentally, as being a thing of common knowledge (see, in this connexion, Ps. lxxvii. 16-19,

Is. li. 9, 10, Job ix. 13, xxvi. 12, 13, xli. 1-34, Ezek. xxix. 3, xxxii. 2), and it appears to be the central part of a song which, as it now stands, is comprised in verses 5-18 of this psalm, for there are in this passage several other very old-world *traits*, especially verses 5-7.[1]

One other example may be given, namely Ps. civ., which is a good illustration of the way in which ancient matter (which must in earlier days have been the subject of song) has been adapted to the requirements of later ages; the first few verses contain echoes of the creation of the heavens, then follow these words (verses 5-9):

> "He founded the earth upon her pillars; she shall not move for evermore.
> Tehom covered her like a garment; upon the hills the waters stood;
> At thy rebuke they fled; at the voices of thy thunder in terror they fled.
> Mountains rose up, valleys sank down into the place which thou didst fix for them.
> A bound thou didst set which they may not pass; they may not return to cover the earth."

Here the reference to the ancient story of Jehovah's victory is sufficiently obvious not to require insisting upon (*cp.* also verse 26). The rest of the psalm deals in the main, with the many blessings which Israel's God has given to His people; all the good things

[1] These are dealt with in the writer's book referred to above, pp. 96-104.

which men enjoy have been given them by Him. The point of importance is that the ancient story of how Jehovah slew the primeval watery monster, Tehom, is here sung. It must have been sung for ages before it was embodied in this hymn of praise; its presence in the psalms which have been referred to can only be explained on the supposition that it had been handed down in song for many generations, because the Jewish doctrine of God underwent a great change after the Exile, the conceptions concerning Jehovah became more spiritualized, and anthropomorphisms were largely toned down. It is inconceivable that psalms composed originally in post-exilic times should have dealt with this antique story of a material combat between Jehovah and Tehom; strong as Babylonian influence was upon Jewish thought, during and after the Exile, the ideas concerning Jehovah, the God of Israel, could not have been influenced in a retrograde direction. It was different when it was a case of songs which had been hallowed by use for many generations among the Israelites; the form of such songs might well undergo change, but their substance would remain, and be adapted to changing circumstances. So that we may conclude that in the few examples which have been considered we have the remains of ancient literature which have, probably enough, gone through more than one process of editing. Compiled from written sources which, as literature, must have had a history behind them, and which were themselves adaptations of previously existing material which embodied some of the traditional beliefs held for ages, and which even during an oral stage must have undergone many modifications—it is not to be wondered at that only fragments have remained. But the ancient songs which told of the mighty deeds of Jehovah in days of old were very precious because they magnified the national God; in later days the conceptions concerning Jehovah's Personality underwent change, which necessitated some modifications in the form of praise offered to Him, and therefore the form in which the old hymns of praise were set was altered; but the *type* was the same. Thus it has come about that only echoes of the early form of hymns of praise are to be discerned in the psalms in question; but the type continued to exist, as it had existed for many centuries.

(*b*) The second type of ancient song to which reference was made was that which commemorated the heroic deeds of ancestors. Songs of this kind were naturally connected with the history of the nation, and we saw that this type, therefore, developed into the historical ode; but it is probable that the two were originally distinct. In the Psalms there are but faint traces of the type in which the heroic deeds of the nation's ancestors are commemorated, see Psalms xcix. 6, 7; cv. 41; cvi. 23, 30; but the historical ode proper is well represented, see *e.g.* Psalms xliv. 1-8; lxxviii., lxxxi., lxxxiii., cv., cvi., cvii., cviii. 7-13, cxiv.; national history thus became incorporated in the Temple hymns. An example of the more specific historical song of triumph, Psalm lxviii., is a magnificent illustration of a type which in earlier days was represented, *e.g.*, by the song in Judges v. On the other hand, Psalms xliv. 9-26, lx. 1-4, cxxxvii. may be instanced as songs of the type of the dirge in 2 Samuel i. 19-27. It is unnecessary to go into details concerning these types, the reading of the psalms in question will illustrate what has been said; they are probably all late in date, but that does not affect the types they represent.

(*c*) It might be thought that folk-songs, such as were sung at harvest and vintage time, represent a type which is not likely to be found in the Psalms; in their old form we shall certainly seek them there in vain. But it must be remembered that such songs were always to some extent expressions of gratitude to Jehovah for His bounty, and as such they would naturally develop into psalms of thanksgiving for material benefits. In Psalm lxv. 9-13, for example, we have a harvest-song which is of striking beauty:

> "Thou visitest the earth, and waterest it, to enrich it;
> The river (better 'brook') of God is full of water.
> Thou preparest corn for them, yea, thus thou preparest it,
> Watering her furrows, settling her ridges;

Thou makest it soft with showers, thou blessest its growth.
Thou crownest the year with thy goodness,
And thy paths drop fatness;
The pastures of the wilderness trickle (with fatness),
And the hills gird themselves with joy.
The hills clothe themselves with flocks,
And the valleys cover themselves with corn;
They shout for joy, and they sing."

This may well be the developed form of an ancient song incorporated into a psalm of later date; it certainly proves that this *type* of song is represented in the Psalms. Another example of this type is to be found in Psalm cxlvii. 7-9, where Jehovah is praised for His gifts of rain and the fruits of the field; and a reminiscence of both a harvest and a vintage song is evidently contained in Psalm civ. 13-15.

(*d*) A large proportion of the Psalms are, to judge from their form and contents, to be regarded rather as prayers intended for private use than as hymns of praise to be used in public worship, and which were, therefore, never meant to be sung and never were sung. Psalm vii., for example, which is probably one of the oldest in the Psalter, is of this nature, so, too, Psalms iii., xiii., xxiii., among the older ones, and many others of later date. That psalms of this nature represent a type, much developed of course, which is of great antiquity, seems to lie almost in the nature of things; for they witness to the inevitable need of man to commune with his Maker; this applies with special force to the Israelites, among whom the religious instinct has always been a marked characteristic. One has only to read such a passage as Judges vi. 12-15, to see how natural, and therefore how common, must have been these individual outpourings of the heart to God. In later times many prayers of this kind became stereotyped, and were ultimately adapted for use for any individual. Their incorporation into the Psalter did not imply that they were intended for public worship, but rather for the use of individuals in the Temple. The custom of going up into the Temple to pray (see Luke xviii. 10 ff.) only reflects what must have been done from time immemorial; before the existence of the Temple the local sanctuaries would have been used for this purpose. Psalms of this kind, therefore, represent a type which may well be regarded as having been in existence in the earliest times (see further Chapter X.)

In the Psalms, then, we must recognise types of songs of praise, and of prayers, which have, in differing forms, been the possession of the Israelites from almost the beginning of their history; and the bulk of them *represent* songs, or prayers, of great antiquity, which have been adapted to the changing circumstances of the times, but which have been altered not so much in substance and context, as in form.

(*e*) Lastly, there are a certain number of psalms which are not adaptations of ancient songs, but which represent an altogether new type brought into existence by new conditions; such are, for example, the "Hallel" group (on these, see pp. 120 f.), the "Songs of Ascents" (see pp. 125 ff.), and others.

CHAPTER VI.

THE POETICAL STRUCTURE OF THE PSALMS.

A BRIEF consideration of Hebrew poetry, especially in reference to the poetical structure of the Psalms, is, apart from the general interest of the subject itself, of importance, because it is of the greatest use in helping to discern what psalms are composite, and thus of throwing some light upon the way in which many of the psalms have been constructed. The rules of Hebrew "metre" are simple, as will be seen; and when the structure of a psalm is broken, which is not difficult to discern on account of the general simplicity of Hebrew "metre," one is able to see at once where and how its original form has been altered. But apart from this, some insight into Hebrew poetical structure—even without any knowledge of Hebrew—is useful, because by means of it one is often enabled to understand better the meaning of a psalm.

§ I. *The Characteristics of Hebrew Poetry.*

Poetry, like music, is a means of expressing the emotions; the former may be said to represent the brain, the latter the heart; the ideal way of giving outward expression to the emotions is by means of the combination of music and poetry. Among cultured peoples these two have become separated to a much larger extent than was the case among less cultivated races, among whom the two are indissoluble; with them poetry is never said, it is always sung. But just as, among these, the term "music" is to be understood in a sense which will not bear comparison with the modern connotation of the word, so it is with poetry. If one listens to a class of children in a National School reciting poetry, two things strike one: the "sing-song," and the rhythm. These are two elementary characteristics which attach to the recitation of poetry. The way in which children *naturally* recite their poetry is an illustration of the method of uncultured man. Again, anyone who reads the attempts which children sometimes make at writing poetry will notice two characteristics which usually assert themselves: the rhythmic element is sufficiently discernable, but the metre is defective. It is primarily the rhythm, corresponding to the "musical" element when the poem is recited, which differentiates poetry from prose; for the essential difference between these two, as far as the form is concerned, is that the expression of emotion, which in prose is continued uninterruptedly, is checked periodically in poetry, as though to set in relief the variations of the emotions expressed. Now the characteristics of the child's poetry represent two elements in Hebrew poetry which are the first to be noticed. Hebrew poetry has no regular *metre*, but its *rhythm* is strongly marked ; the constant number of syllables to a line, to which we are accustomed in modern poetry, is not found in Hebrew poetry ; so long as the rhythm is distinct the number of syllables in a line is immaterial. This can be seen in the following transliteration :—

Ladonái ha'áretz umĕlo'áh (ten syllables)
To the Lórd the eárth and its fúlness
Tébel wĕjóshbē báh (six syllables)
The wórld and the dwéllers thereín
Ki hú 'al-yamím yĕsadáh (eight syllables)
For Hé on the wáters hath sét it
Wĕ 'ál-nĕharóth yĕkonéhĕh (ten syllables)
And on rívers estáblished ít.[1]

It will be seen at once here that while the number of syllables varies in each line, the rhythmic three beats to each line is quite distinct. The principle embodied in this example holds good for all Hebrew poetry whatever the number of "beats" to a line, and that there are different modes of this kind will be seen presently. Hebrew poetry, therefore, is not based on quantity, but on accentuated syllables ; it is true that there are other accents than those indicated in the example given above, but the minor accents are disregarded as far as the rhythm is concerned, and only

[1] Ps. xxiv. 1, 2.

the important accents come into consideration;[1] this holds good of all Old Testamentt Hebrew poetry. From what has been said it follows that in Hebrew poetry we are not to look for lines of corresponding lengths; where the main desire is to express thought or emotion in the most telling way that could be, symmetrical lines did not come into consideration.

Another characteristic of Hebrew poetry is that the ends of the lines do not rhyme; it happens often enough that lines end with similar-sounding syllables, as, for example, in the quotation given above, in which each line ends with *—ah;* this is, however, due to the form of the Hebrew suffixes, not to the desire to make a rhyme. Instead of rhyme similar-sounding words occur (not necessarily at the end of a line); thus in Ps. cxlviii., *e.g.*, each of the verses 2-4 begins with *Hallelúhu* "Praise Him;" and verses 3-5 begin respectively thus:

"*Hallĕlúhu shemesh wĕyaɂéach* . . ."
"Praise Him, *sun*[2] and moon . . ."
"*Hallĕlúhu shĕmē hashamáim* . . ."
"Praise Him, *Heaven of Heavens* . . ."
"*Yĕhállĕlu 'eth-shém 'Adonái* . . ."
"Let them praise the *name* of the Lord . . ."

[1] *Cp.* Ugolino, *Thesaurus* xxxii., pp. 389f., where he says, after enumerating the accents in the Psalms: Nota hoc loco accentus hosce musicos non ad canendum tantum, sed ad pulchram pronunciationem esse institutos, ut scias scilicet, ubi suspendere spiritum, quo loco versum distinguere, ubi comma figere, ubi colon apponere debeas, ubi versus claudatur, ubi incipiat, quid lentius, celerius, concitatius lenius denique ac temperatius tardiusque sit efferendum.

[2] These italicized words are the similar-sounding ones in Hebrew.

Moreover, many examples of alliteration could be given; one of the most striking is to be found in Ps. cxxii. 6:

Sha'alu shelom Jerushalaim yishlaiu 'ohabaik; this is reproduced by the English version: "*P*ray for the *p*eace of Jerusalem, may they *p*rosper that love thee."

Again, a favourite device in Hebrew poetry is the use of *Catchwords;* for example, it strikes the eye at once when one sees three successive lines (Ps. xiii. 2, 3), beginning with *'ad-anah*, "How long"; that is, as it were, the motto of the psalm. Striking, again, is the catchword *Qol-Adonai*, "The voice of the Lord," which occurs no less than eight times in Ps. xxix. Somewhat similar to these catchwords, as indicating the main idea of a psalm, only more elaborate, are the *Refrains* which are characteristic of some psalms; for example, in Ps. xlii. 5, 11, xliii. 5 (the two originally formed one psalm), a refrain is repeated three times: "Why art thou cast down, my soul? And why art thou disquieted within me? Hope in God, for I shall yet praise Him, (who is) the health of my countenance, and my God." More pronounced is the refrain, repeated twenty-six times, of Ps. cxxxvi., "For His mercy endureth for ever;" this refrain occurs also in the psalm which is inserted in the Hebrew of *Ecclesiasticus* after li. 12; it is repeated fourteen times.

Lastly, Hebrew poetry is characterised by the use of archaic words; these consist not only of nouns, but also of prepositions, suffixes, and case-endings.

§ II. *Forms of Hebrew Poetry.*

The individual lines in Hebrew poetry belong to different classes according to their "measure," or, in other words, according to the number of " beats " in a line. These classes are clearly defined, and are as follows :—

(*a*) The *Trimeter;* this is the most common measure in the Psalter, and consists of three rhythmic beats to a line, viz. :

Adonaí, mah-rabbú zaraí
Lord, hów are my fóes multipliéd,
Rabbím kamím 'alaí
There are mány that ríse against mé.[1]

(*b*) The *Tetrameter;* this measure occurs far less frequently in the Psalter, it consists of four rhythmic beats to the line, viz. :

Hoshí'ah Adonai ki-gamár chasíd
Save Lórd for the gódly man ceáseth to bé,
Ki-pássu 'ĕmuním mibĕnē 'adám
The faíthful have faíled from the sóns of mén.[2]

Not infrequently in this class a *caesura* comes in the middle of the line, *i.e.*, it is cut into two divisions, each division having two beats; a good example of this is the following :—

'Ad-'ánah Adonaí || tishkachéni nézach
How lóng, O Lórd || wilt Thou éver forgét me ?[3]

[1] Ps. iii. 2, *cp.* also Ps. xxiv. 1, 2, cited above. [2] Ps. xii. 1.
[3] Psalm xiii. 2.

This *caesura* is usually found in lines of ten or more syllables.

(*c*) The *Pentameter;* the five beats to a line is a measure which occurs slightly oftener in the Psalter; it always has the *caesura*, sometimes after second, but more frequently after the third beat, *e.g.*:—

'Ashré nĕsúi peshá' || kĕsúi chăta'áh
Blést the forgív'n of tréspass || whose sín is cóver'd.[1]

(*d*) The *Hexameter;* this measure has six beats in a line, the position of the *caesura* varies, coming mostly after the third beat, though sometimes after the second; there are instances of two *caesuras* in one line, dividing it into three sections of two beats each. A good instance of the hexameter is Psalm cxxi., of which the first verse runs:—

'Essá 'eynaí 'el-heharím || me'áyin yabó 'ezrí
I will líft mine éyes to the hílls; || from whénce will cóme my hélp?

(*e*) The *Kinah* measure; this is the measure proper to elegiac poetry in Hebrew; its usual form is a line of three beats followed by a shorter one of two beats, *e.g.*, Psalm xix., 8-10, contains this measure; the first line of verse 8 runs:—

Toráth 'Adonaí tĕmímah—mĕshíbath néphesh
The Láw of the Lórd is pérfect—restóring the soúl.

[1] Psalm xxxii. 1.

Other examples occur in Amos v. 2, Ezek. xix. 1, and almost the whole *Book of Lamentations*.[1] These different measures are not necessarily confined to special psalms, two or more are sometimes represented in the same psalm; for example, the first four lines of Psalm xxiii. are trimeters, the second four tetrameters, and the last four pentameters. Other psalms have still greater variety. But as a general rule a particular metre runs through one psalm.

We have dealt with the varying measures of the *lines* in Hebrew poetry; we have next to consider what in modern poetry corresponds to the *verse;* for this purpose we must put aside altogether the system of verse-divisions as found in the English Psalter, whether in the Bible or in the Prayer Book Version, which is very misleading.

We have in Hebrew poetry, and especially in the Psalms, groups of lines, or "stichs,"[2] which form something corresponding roughly to the verse in modern poetry. These verses, or "strophes,"[3] vary according to the number of lines they contain. *Monostichs*, verses consisting of a single line, do not come into consideration because they do not, properly speaking, constitute a poetical verse; if, however, such

[1] On this *Kinah*-measure see further Budde in the *New World* for March, 1893, and in the *Zeitschrift für die alttestamentliche Wissenschaft*, ii. 45.

[2] From the Greek *stichos*, "a row," or "line."

[3] From the Greek *strophé*, lit. "a turning," *i.e.*, the part of a song sung in turning from the right to the left of the orchestra, in the Greek drama.

a psalm as cxlv. could be said to have strophes we should have to define each of them as a *monostich*, because each individual line is a self-contained unity. Strophes of this kind occur but rarely in the Psalter or elsewhere. *Distichs*, verses consisting of two lines, abound in the Book of *Proverbs*, *e.g.*:

> "The fear of the Lord is the beginning of knowledge;
> But the foolish despise wisdom and instruction."

There are but few of these in the Psalter, some examples occur in Psalms xiv.:

> "The scorners say in their heart, there is no God;
> Corrupt are they, shameful in act, not one does good" (v. 1).

> "The Lord looked from heaven upon the sons of men,
> To see if any were wise, and seeking God" (v. 2).

And so on to the end of verse six, the last being a tristich. Like distichs, *tristichs*, three lines to a verse, are rare in the Psalter (see xiv. 7 as an instance). By far the most usual form of verse in the Psalter is the *tetrastich*, four lines to the verse; one out of a great many may be given, Ps. iii. 1, 2:—

> "Lord, how many are my adversaries,
> Many that rise against me,
> Many that say of my soul:
> 'No salvation for him in his God.'"

The whole psalm is divided in this way. There are

a certain number of *pentastichs*, five lines to a verse, but more frequent are the *hexastichs*, six lines to a verse, in the Psalter. A good example of this is the first psalm, which consists of two hexastichs, with a tetrastich dividing them. *Heptastichs*, seven lines to a verse, are rare; one of the best examples is Ps. ii., which is made up of four of these. There are also verses with eight, and more, lines; but these do not occur often. Some of the psalms have verses with varying numbers of lines.

The number of verses, or *strophes*, which are combined to make up a song, differs considerably according to the content of the song. Some of the psalms, for example, contain only a single strophe, such as most of the "Songs of Ascents," or "Pilgrim Psalms" (cxx.-cxxxiv.); the most usual number of strophes to a psalm is two, three, and four; the longer psalms have, of course, a larger number; Ps. lxxviii., for example, has twenty tetrastichs; other psalms contain verses varying from five to eleven in number.

§ III. *Parallelism.*

A characteristic of Hebrew poetry which must be specially dealt with is the variety of Parallelisms with which it abounds. These cannot be appreciated unless examples are quoted; it will be best, therefore, to mention the name of each variety, and give one illustration of each.

(*a*) *Synonymous Parallelism.* This is the commonest

form; it is the kind in which the second line repeats, in effect, what has been said in the first, only it puts it in a different way, *e.g.* Ps. i. 2:—

> "But his delight is in the law of the Lord,
> And in His law doth he meditate day and night."

(*b*) *Antithetic Parallelism.* In this case the second line expresses the contrast, or the antithesis, to what is said in the first, *e.g.*, Ps. i. 6:

> "For the Lord knoweth the way of the righteous;
> But the way of the wicked shall perish."

(*c*) *Complementary Parallelism.* In this type of parallelism one line is the complement of the other; neither line is complete without the other, as a rule; but a large variety of this type is found, and sometimes, though a line may be complete in itself, the thought expressed is enhanced or emphasized by what the second line says. Under this heading comes, also, the couplet which offers a comparison; this variety is found mostly in the Wisdom-literature. A few examples, illustrating several of the varieties, may be given:

> O Lord my God, in Thee do I take refuge,
> Save me from all that pursue me, and deliver me."
> (Ps. vii. 2.)

Here the second line is the complement of the first.

> "Shew us thy mercy, O Lord,
> And grant us thy salvation."
> (Ps. lxxxv. 7.)

In this case the second line is an enhancement of the first.

> "As the hart panteth after the water-brooks,
> So panteth my soul after thee, O God."
> (Ps. xlii. 1.)

This couplet is an example of a comparison.

> "Make glad the soul of thy servant, O Lord,
> For unto thee I lift up my soul."
> (Ps. lxxxvi. 4).

The first line here gives the reason for what the second says.

There are other varieties of "complementary" parallelisms, but the examples cited show the genera nature of this type.

(*d*) *Introverted Parallelism.* This is the name given to those cases in which, for example, the first line corresponds to the fourth, and the second to the third; different varieties of this type also occur; the following is an example:

> "To thee, Jehovah, I cry: and to the Lord I make supplication.
> What profit is there in my blood when I go down to the pit?
> Shall dust praise thee, shall it declare thy truth?
> Hear, Jehovah, and be gracious to me: Jehovah be my helper."

In this case it will be seen that the first and fourth lines are parallel, while the second and third are, as it were, in parenthesis, but also parallel.

§ IV. *Acrostic Poems.*

These constitute an interesting element in Hebrew poetry; one of the most striking examples is Psalm cxix., in which each line of each division begins with the same letter, running through the whole alphabet in order. Other examples, of a less elaborate character, are Psalms xxv., xxxiv., xxxvii., cxlv., and others; also Ecclus. li. 13-29, though this is incomplete in its present form.

Generally speaking, Hebrew Poetry may be divided into three great classes: Lyric, Gnomic, and Elegiac Poetry; the two former greatly preponderate. By *Lyric* poetry is meant the expression of emotions of every kind, joyous and sorrowful; everything that expresses the feelings of the individual. *Gnomic* poetry deals with conduct of life, and ethics generally. The *Book of Lamentations* is the great example of *Elegiac* poetry. The *Epos* and the *Drama* seem to have been foreign to the Hebrew genius; they are only very slightly represented, and that in a modified form, in ancient Hebrew poetry. Some scanty remnants of the former are to be discerned in some of the Psalms (see *e.g.*, lxxiv. 12-15, lxxxix. 8-10). The *Song of Songs*, and the *Book of Job* are the only examples of the latter, and these only in a modified sense; "in structure the Book of Job is of the nature of a drama, and may be termed a dramatic poem; its principal parts are constructed in the form of a dialogue, in which characters are introduced advocating in their speeches different theories of providence, and so contributing to the development of a common theme."[1]

[1] Driver, *The Book of Job*, p. x.

CHAPTER VII.

THE PSALMS IN THE TEMPLE WORSHIP.

§ I. *The Musical Accompaniment to the Psalms in the Temple Worship.*

It is not infrequently said that the Psalter was the Hymn-book of the Second Temple; but the statement is not strictly accurate; for while there can be little doubt that all the psalms which were sung in the Temple worship are contained in the Psalter, it is reasonably certain that it contains in addition a good many which were not, and were never intended to be, sung at public worship.

Our authorities for the use of the Psalms in the Temple are the Old Testament and some Mishnic tractates, as well as scattered references in the *Gemara*. The *data* given in the books of *Chronicles* refer only to post-exilic usage,[1] indeed, so far as the use of the Psalms is concerned there are only scanty details as to what was done in pre-exilic times. In 1 Kings viii. there is a long account of the service at the dedication of

[1] On this, see Büchler, *Zur Geschichte der Tempel Musik und der Tempel Psalmen*, in the "Zeitschrift fur die alt-test. Wissenschaft," xix. pp. 133 ff.

Solomon's Temple; here prayer and sacrifice are very prominent; but it is inconceivable that no music and no singing of psalms took place. When we read in 1 Kings viii. 1-6 of the assembling of "the elders of Israel, and all the heads of the tribes, the princes of the fathers' houses of the children of Israel, unto King Solomon in Jerusalem, to bring up the ark of the covenant of the Lord out of the city of David. . . . And the priests brought in the ark of the covenant of the Lord unto its place, into the oracle of the house, to the most holy place . . . ," we are irresistibly reminded of 2 Samuel vi. 1 ff. where the account is given of David gathering the people together in order to bring the ark of God up to the city of David. It is there said: "And David, and all the house of Israel played before the Lord with all manner of instruments made of fir wood, and with harps, and with psalteries, and with timbrels, and with castanets, and with cymbals;" and again in verse 15: "So David and all the house of Israel brought up the ark of the Lord with shouting, and with the sound of the trumpet." It is impossible to believe that the earlier usage was not followed by Solomon; and we may take it for granted that songs of praise, accompanied by musical instruments,[1] were a leading feature in this service; nor were

[1] With the exception of the blowing of the trumpet and of the *shôphar* (*cp.* Numbers xxxi. 6, Joshua vi. 4 ff.) the idea of instrumental music apart from singing was foreign to the Israelites; in Hebrew, musical instruments are called *Kělē hashshir*, "instruments of song," and only come into consideration as forming an accompaniment to song.

they likely to have been wanting subsequently in the Temple worship. But while the fact is incontrovertible, the details of what was sung during this early period are wanting.

The tradition that David organized the Levitical singers into three classes under the leadership respectively of Asaph, Heman, and Jeduthun,[1] accords with the manifold evidence of David's love for music. Of these three, Asaph is always mentioned first, and he seems to have occupied the position of leader of the music in the Temple generally. In later days these three names became the designations of guilds of Temple-singers and musicians,[2] but it is more than probable that the office which Asaph was the first to fill continued as long as the Temple stood. We are told in later days of a Temple official whose special duty it was to superintend the psalmody;[3] there were, under him, a large number of musicians, including singers and instrumentalists; these had to accompany the daily burnt-offering as well as the solemn festival services with singing of Psalms and playing on stringed instruments[4]—but we shall return to this later on. An interesting account of the musical liturgical service is given in 2 Chron. xxix. 26-30, the reference is to the

[1] Sometimes called Ethan.

[2] *Cp.* the term "sons of Asaph," in 1 Chron. xxv. 1; 2 Chron. v. 12, xxxv. 15; Ezra ii. 41; Neh. vii. 44.

[3] See further Herzog, *Real-Encycl. für Bibel und Talmud*, x. pp. 387 ff.

[4] Mishna, *Yoma* iii. 11, *Tamid* vii. 3

Passover service: "And the Levites stood with the instruments of David, and the priests with the trumpets. And Hezekiah commanded to offer the burnt-offering upon the altar. And when the burnt-offering began, the song of the Lord began also, and the trumpets, together with the instruments of David, King of Israel. And all the congregation worshipped, and the singers sang, and the trumpeters sounded; all this continued until the burnt-offering was finished. And when they had made an end of offering, the King and all that were present with him bowed themselves and worshipped. Moreover, Hezekiah the King and the princes commanded the Levites to sing praises unto the Lord with the words of David, and of Asaph the seer. And they sang praises with gladness, and they bowed their heads and worshipped."[1] When it is said here: "The song of the Lord began also, and the trumpets, together with the instruments of David," the reference is to the singing of psalms with the accompaniment of the stringed instruments, *i.e.* harps and lutes; the music of the Temple is constantly spoken of as *neginah,* which means the music of stringed instruments,[2] and it was, with the exception of the cymbals, generally speaking, restricted to harps and lutes. It was only on certain special occasions that there was an accompaniment of flutes, viz. on the two first days of

[1] See also Ecclus. l. 15-21.

[2] *Cp.* the titles of Pss. iv., vi., liv., lv., lxi., lxvii., lxxvi.; Is. xxxviii. 20; Heb. iii. 19.

Passover, the first day of unleavened bread, Pentecost, and the eight days of the Feast of Tabernacles;[1] "quite in accordance with the social character of these feasts, the flute was also used by the festive pilgrim-bands on their journey to Jerusalem, to accompany the 'Psalms of Degrees,' or rather 'Ascents,'[2] sung on such occasions. . . . In the Temple not less than two nor more than twelve flutes were allowed."[3] Trumpets were, as a rule, only used for the purpose of giving signals at certain places during the service; they were blown by the priests; in 2 Chron. v. 11-13, however, it is stated that the trumpets accompanied the singing, this is exceptional.[4] This passage is interesting from another point of view, it runs: "And it came to pass, when the priests were come out of the holy place . . . it came even to pass, when the trumpeters and singers were even as one, to make one sound to be heard in praising and thanking the Lord, and when they lifted up their voice with the trumpets and cymbals and instruments of song, and praised the Lord . . .";

[1] *Cp.* the Mishna, *'Arakhin* ii. 3, 4.

[2] *Cp.* Is. xxx. 29: "Ye shall have a song as in the night when a holy feast is kept; and gladness of heart, as when one goeth with a pipe to come into the mountain of the Lord."

[3] Edersheim, *The Temple and its Services*, p. 56 (1874); he adds, quoting Leyrer (art. "Music" in Herzog's *Encycl.*): "The flute was used in Alexandria to accompany the hymns at the love-feasts of the early Christians, up to the year 190, when Clement of Alexandria introduced the harp in its place."

[4] In later times it appears to have become more usual to use trumpets in the worship itself, see 1 Macc. iv. 40, v. 33.

the Chronicler evidently regards this *unison* between the singing and the instrumental accompaniment as the ideal way of rendering the vocal and instrumental *ensemble.*

We have, further, in the Talmud and elsewhere, some few more or less reliable *data* of the usage in later times concerning instrumental music in the Temple. According to the Talmud, *'Arakhin* 10*b*, 11*a*, there was in use in the Herodian Temple a *Magrēphah*,[1] which accompanied the singing; this was a wind instrument, and was apparently, a kind of primitive organ. It is said to have been able to produce a hundred different tones; this latter is evidently somewhat of an exaggeration. Then again, Maimonides (*Kĕlē hammikdah* iii.) tells us that there was in the Herodian Temple an orchestra consisting of from two to six players on the *nabla* ("harp"), six who played the *kinnor* ("lyre"), and one who struck the cymbals; to these were added, according to the Talmud, from two to twelve flute-players, and two trumpeters.[2] The extravagant praise accorded elsewhere in the Talmud to the musical element in the Temple-worship cannot always be taken seriously.

[1] See further Ugolini (*Thesaurus* xxii. pp. 353 ff.) who says the Magrēphah had thirteen pipes and two bellows; an illustration is given on p. 371, see also pp. 1121 ff. It was used, according to Maimonides, in order to summon the priests to worship, and the Levites to their song during certain parts of the services, *cp.* Edersheim, *Op. cit.* p. 140 note.

[2] *Cp.* Benzinger, *Op. cit.* p. 598.

As regards the singers[1] themselves, it is sometimes stated that these included women at one time; this is said to be gathered from Ps. lxviii. 24-25: "They have seen thy goings, O God, even the goings of my God, my King, into the sanctuary. The singers went before, the minstrels followed after, in the midst of the damsels playing with timbrels."[2] More pointed, however, is Ezra ii. 65, where mention is made of "two hundred singing men and singing women," and Neh. vii. 67, . . . "and they had two hundred forty and five singing men and singing women." The musical direction *'al 'alamoth* (see 1 Chron. xv. 20, Pss. ix. 1. xlvi, 1, xlviii. 15) means literally "according to" or "after the manner of maidens." This certainly seems to point to women's voices. According to the, probably correct, emendation of part of Amos viii. 3, this passage should be read: "Then will the women-singers in the Temple howl." In later times women's voices were no longer heard in the Service, Levitical singers alone being employed; in the Temple of

[1] Called in Hebrew *Mĕshorĕrim*, so often mentioned in the books of Ezra and Nehemiah; in Greek ψαλτῳδοί, so *e.g.* in Ecclus. xlvii. 9; they were originally distinct from the Levites, but according to the Mishna the Temple musicians were synonymous with "Levites," *e.g. Tamid* vii. 3, *'Arakhin* ii. 6.

[2] This passage must not, however, be pressed, for it is doubtful whether the reference is to actual worship; it seems to be rather a description of a procession on its way to worship, and accompanied by damsels who would presumably remain behind when the actual place of worship was reached. See what has been said on, p. 59.

Herod Levite boys' voices became a regular feature in worship.[1]

§. II. *The Psalms used in the Temple-Worship.*

We come next to consider the actual Psalms which were used in the worship of the Temple. It will be most convenient if we deal first with the psalms used in the daily services, then with those sung during the services on the Sabbath, and finally with the special Psalms chosen for the Festivals.

(*a*) *The Psalms in the Daily Services.*

During the daily sacrifices[2] the priests blew on their trumpets; while the burnt-offerings was being presented the Levites sang and played,[3] and after the sacrifices had been offered, one of the priests struck the cymbals. This was the signal for the Levitical Choir to sing the psalm for the day, which was accompanied by stringed instruments. This special psalm varied with each day of the week. In the Mishna[4] the daily psalms, together with the reasons why they were chosen, are given as follows:—

On the first day of the week, xxiv., "The earth is the

[1] See further below, on the singing of the Psalms in the ancient Synagogue.

[2] *i.e.* The burnt-offerings, the sin and trespass-offerings, the peace-offerings, and the drink-offering.

[3] It is not stated what precise psalms were sung here.

[4] *Tamid* vii., and Babylonian Talmud, *Roth Hashshana* 30*b*, 31*a*. *Sopherim* xviii. 1.

Lord's, and the fulness thereof," sung in commemoration of the first day of Creation. On the second day, xlviii., "Great is the Lord, and highly to be praised"; on the third, lxxxii., "God standeth in the congregation"; on the fourth, xciv., "O Lord, Thou God to whom vengeance belongeth"; on the fifth, lxxxi., "Sing aloud unto God our strength"; on the sixth, xciii., "The Lord reigneth, He is clothed with majesty"; and on the Sabbath, xcii., "It is a good thing to give thanks unto the Lord." With the exception of the first it is difficult to see any connexion between the reason of the choice of the particular psalm, and its contents. In most cases, the third and fifth day only excepted, the Septuagint, in the titles of the respective psalms, corroborates what the Mishna states as to these being the special daily psalms. Regarding the last, the Hebrew Bible also mentions in the title, "A Song for the Sabbath day." According to *Tamid* vii. 3, the singing of the psalm for the day was commenced when the priest began to pour out the drink-offering; but the sources are somewhat ambiguous regarding the time at which this psalm was sung. On the other hand, it seems certain that it was sung in three parts, after each of which there was a pause in the singing and music; during this pause, two of the priests blew their trumpets, this was the signal for the congregation to fall down and pray. Here, again, we must deplore the want of more precise information; for we are not told whether this was silent prayer, or whether it was offered by one of the officiating ministers on behalf of the worshippers, nor how long the pause lasted. One point comes out strongly, namely, that the sacrifices were the really important element in the worship, while the singing of psalms and the music were both intended primarily to be merely the setting of this central act of worship.

(*b*) *The Psalms in the Sabbath Services.*

The sacrifices offered on the Sabbath were at each service (morning and evening) as many as those offered at the daily morning and evening services together.[1] It is, therefore, to be presumed that the praise portion, *i.e.* the singing of psalms with their musical accompaniment, was likewise fuller; but direct evidence as to this is not forthcoming. The only definite statement that we have is that at the pouring-out of the drink-offering at the usual morning sacrifice, the Levites sang the special psalm for the Sabbath, xcii., just as at the week-day services; this was, in like manner, also sung in three sections—a liturgical psalm was usually divided into three parts[2]—at the close of each section the priests blew three times upon their trumpets, and the people fell down and worshipped.[3] In addition to this we are also told that "at the close of the additional Sabbath sacrifice, when the drink-offering was brought, the Levites

[1] *Cp.* Num. xxviii. 9, 10; this is also mentioned by Josephus *Antiq.* III. x. 1.

[2] So the Mishna, *Sukkah* iv. 5.

[3] *Cp. Tamid* vii 3.

sang the "Song of Moses" in Deut. xxxii. This "hymn" was divided into six portions, for as many Sabbaths (verses 1-6, 7-12, 13-18, 19-28, 29-39, 40-end). Each portion was sung in three sections with threefold blasts of the priests' trumpets, the people worshipping at each pause. If a Sabbath and a "new moon" fell on the same day, the Sabbath hymn was sung in preference to that for the new moon; if a feast-day fell on the Sabbath, the Sabbath sacrifice was offered before that prescribed for the feast-day. At the evening sacrifice on the Sabbath the song of Moses in in Exod. xv. was sung."[1]

(*c*) *The Festival Psalms.* The most important of these was the "Hallel." The "Hallel" is the name given in Rabbinical writings to the six psalms cxiii.-cxviii.;[2] these were always considered as forming one whole. "Hallel" means "Praise," and the name is given on account of the oft-recurring word "Hallelujah" ("Praise ye the Lord") in these Psalms. The "Hallel" was sung on the following occasions:—

At the Feast of Passover.

When the Passover lambs had been slain two rows of

[1] Edersheim, *Op. cit.* pp. 158 f.

[2] Called the "Egyptian Hallel" to distinguish it from the "Great Hallel" (Pss. cxx.-cxxxvi.), and from Pss. cxlvi.-cxlviii. Tradition is undecided as to whether these really did form the "Hallel"; see Hamburger *Op. cit.*, art. *Hallel.* According to Bar Kapara, Ps. cxxxvi. constituted the "Great Hallel"; in *Berakhoth* 56 *a* Pss. cxiii., cxiv. are called the "Egyptian Hallel," see Müller's notes on his edition o *Sopherim*, p. 288, and *cp.* the Midrash *Pesikta* 117 *a*, 118 *a*.

priests were drawn up in the Court of the Priests, in which the great altar stood, and received into gold and silver bowls the blood from the lambs which the head of each family had to offer at this Feast; these bowls were passed up to the officiating priest at the great altar; as he received each bowl he emptied it out at the base of the altar, and then handed the empty bowl back. This ceremony lasted from the ninth till the eleventh hour (*i.e.* 3-5 p.m.).[1] Now it was during this ceremony that the "Hallel" was sung by the Levites. The people repeated the first clause of each of the six psalms, and after every other clause or line they shouted "Hallelujah"; when they came to the last of the six (Psalm cxviii.) they repeated not only the first clause, and shouted "Hallelujah" after each clause, but also repeated after the Levites the three clauses contained in verses 25, 26:

> "Save now, we beseech Thee, O Lord;
> O Lord, we beseech Thee, send us now prosperity.
> Blessed is he that cometh in the name of the Lord."

The "Hallel" was repeated in this manner until the whole ceremony was completed.

There was also, according to Müller,[2] a special Psalm (cxxxv.) sung at this Feast; this was chosen

[1] The number of lambs sacrificed must have been very large; Josephus (*Bell. Jud.* VI. ix. 3) tells us that on one occasion 256,000 were offered allowing, even, for the obvious exaggeration, there must have been a very large number.

[2] See his note on *Sopherim* xviii. 2.

on account of the reference to the deliverance from Egypt in verses 8, 9. We are not told, however, at what particular part of the celebration this psalm was sung.

At the Feast of Tabernacles.

The first ceremony during this Feast which comes into consideration in the present connexion is the water-libation. "The libation of water[1] was a ceremony to which grave importance was attached. The custom may perhaps be traced to the very ancient practice of drawing and pouring out water at religious services as reported in 1 Sam. vii. 6. It is regarded as symbolic of rain[2] . . . A prayer for rain is recited on the eighth day."[3] The ceremony was as follows:[4] A priest went from the Temple with a golden pitcher to Siloah; he filled it there with water, and returned with it through the water-gate. As he entered the gate the people sang: "Therefore with joy shall ye draw water out of the wells of salvation."[5] This water was then poured out as a libation upon the altar, and together with it a libation of wine; trumpets were sounded while this was being done. Thereupon the Temple music began, and the "Hallel" was sung in the same way as at the Feast of Passover. On this occasion, however, it was sung to the accompaniment of flutes, excepting on the Sabbath, and on the first day

[1] Described in the Mishna, *Sukkah* iv. 1. [2] See Zech. xiv. 16, 17.

[3] Friedmann in the *Jewish Encycl.* xi. 660*b*.

[4] *Sukkah* iv. 9, 10. [5] Is. xii. 3.

of the Feast,[1] because these were regarded as especially holy. When, in singing this, the Levites came to the words: "O give thanks unto the Lord" (Ps. cxviii. 1), and to the words: "Save now, we beseech Thee,[2] O Lord . . . blessed is he that cometh in the name of the Lord" (Ps. cxviii. 25, 26), and again to the concluding words: "O give thanks unto the Lord, for He is good"—all the people shook their *lulabs*[3] towards the altar.

After the sacrifices had been offered on each of the seven days of this Feast the priests marched in procession round the altar and again sang Ps. cxviii. 25, "Save now . . ." On the seventh day a sevenfold procession round the altar took place. This was also done at all the great Feasts after the daily sacrifices had been offered.[4]

Psalms were also sung at another ceremony during this Feast, a ceremony of which it is said that whoever has not seen it has never seen a real Feast.[5] "In the brilliantly illuminated court of the women, before the assembled multitude occupying the double gallery

[1] Originally it lasted seven days; Josephus (*Antiq.* VIII., iv. 1), speaks of it as an eight-day Feast; in the modern Synagogue it lasts for nine days.

[2] The Hebrew for, "Save (now), we beseech Thee," is *Hoshi'ah-na* = "Hosanna;" see Matt. xxi. 6-11, John xii. 12-16.

[3] The *lulab* is the "palm-branch" which was, and is still, used during this Feast; this is done in accordance with the command given in Lev. xxiii. 40, "And ye shall take you on the first day the fruit of goodly trees, branches of palm-trees . . ."

[4] *Sukkah* iv. 2. [5] *Sukkah* v. 1.

erected by the priests and Levites, the most prominent Israelites took part in a torch-dance, reciting at the same time hymns and songs of praise. Meanwhile, on the steps of the inner court stood the Levites singing Pss. cxx.-cxxxiv.,[1] accompanied by various musical instruments. The celebration continued till cockcrow, when the two priests at the Nicanor gate sounded the signal, and the crowd departed, facing about, however, at the eastern, when the priests recited, "Our forefathers in this place turned their backs on the altar of God, and their faces to the east, worshipping the sun; but we turn to God."[2] This ceremony has been discontinued since the destruction of the Temple, 70 A.D.

At the Feast of Weeks.

During the offering of various sacrifices[3] prescribed for this Feast, the "Hallel" was sung; it was accompanied by one flute. What gave special charm to it on this occasion was that the sons of the Levites sang it together with their fathers. The part taken by the congregation was the same as at the Passover Feast.

At the Feast of Dedication.

In 1 Macc. iv. 54 we are told that the Dedication of the Temple by Judas Maccabæus, after its profanation

[1] Mishna, *Middoth* ii. 5; these are the so-called "Songs of Ascents," or "Pilgrim Songs," see below § iii.

[2] Friedmann, *Op. cit.* p. 661 *b.; cp.* Ezek. viii. 15, 16, *Sukkah* v. 1-4.

[3] See Num. xxviii. 26-31.

by Antiochus Epiphanes, was celebrated with "songs and citherns, and harps and cymbals." We know from other sources that the "Hallel" was sung at this Feast[1]; therefore, it seems certain that the "songs" spoken of in this passage refer to this. Furthermore, the title of Ps. xxx. states definitely that it was a song sung at the Dedication of the House (of God), so that clearly this psalm also belongs to those which were used at this Feast.

At the New Moons.

The New Moon was celebrated in the Temple by the offering of special sacrifices,[2] and by the blowing of trumpets by the priests.[3] We have no *data* as to whether any psalms[4] were sung at the ordinary New Moon Festivals, but the celebration in the seventh month was regarded as a more sacred Feast. A special Psalm (lxxxi.) was appointed to be sung on this occasion[5]; it was sung by the priests and Levites at the pouring-out of the drink-offering; there was also a special Psalm (xxix.) for the evening sacrifice.

§ III. *The Songs of Ascents.*

The fifteen Psalms, cxx.-cxxxiv. are called "Songs of Ascents," or "Pilgrim Songs," because they were

[1] *E.g.* in the Babylonian Talmud, *Shabbath* 21 *b*.

[2] See Num. xxviii. 11-15.

[3] See Num. x. 10.

[4] Later on, in the Synagogue, the "Hallel" was sung at New Moons.

[5] If the Feast fell on the fifth day of the week, which already had this as its special psalm, it was repeated from verse 6 (verse 7 in the Hebrew Bible).

sung by those who came up every year to Jerusalem for the three great festivals, in accordance with the command given in Deut. xvi. 16, "Three times in a year shall all thy males appear before the Lord thy God in the place which He shall choose; in the feast of unleavened bread,[1] and in the Feast of Weeks,[2] and in the Feast of Tabernacles; and they shall not appear before the Lord empty." Edersheim's graphic account of one of these pilgrimages is worth quoting in full[3]: "The journey was always to be made slowly, for the pilgrimage was to be a joy and a privilege, not a toil or weariness. In the morning, as the golden sunlight tipped the mountains of Moab, the stationary man of the district, who was the leader, summoned the ranks of the procession in the words of Jeremiah xxxi. 6: 'Arise ye, and let us go up to Zion, and unto Jehovah our God.' To which the people replied, as they formed and moved onwards, in the appropriate language of Ps. cxxxii.: 'I was glad when they said unto me, Let us go into the house of Jehovah.' First went one who played the pipe; then followed a sacrificial bullock, destined for a peace-offering, his horns gilt, and garlanded with olive-branches; next came the multitude, some carrying the baskets with the first-fruits, others singing the Psalms, which many writers suppose to have been specially destined for that service, and hence to have been called 'the Songs of Ascents'; in our Authorized Version, 'the

[1] *I.e.* Passover. [2] *I.e.* Pentecost. [3] *Op. cit.* pp. 337 ff.

Psalms of Degrees.' The poorer brought their gifts in wicker baskets, which afterwards belonged to the officiating priests; the richer theirs in baskets of silver and gold, which were given to the Temple treasury. . . . . And so they passed through the length and breadth of the land, everywhere wakening the echoes of praise. As they entered the city, they sang Psalm cxxii. 2: 'Our feet stand within thy gates, O Jerusalem.' A messenger had preceded them to announce their approach, and a deputation from the Temple, consisting of priests, Levites, and treasurers, varying in numbers according to the importance of the place from which the procession came, had gone out to receive them. In the streets of Jerusalem each one came out to welcome them, with shouts of 'Brethren of such a place' (naming it) 'ye come to peace; welcome, ye come in peace, ye bring peace, and peace be upon you!' As they reached the Temple Mount, each one, whatever his rank or condition, took one of the baskets on his shoulder, and they ascended, singing that appropriate hymn, 'Praise ye Jehovah! praise God in His sanctuary; praise Him in the firmament of His power. . . .' (Psalm cl.). As they entered the courts of the Temple itself, the Levites intoned Psalm xxx.: 'I will extol Thee, O Jehovah; for Thou hast lifted me up, and hast not made my foes to rejoice over me. . . .' Then the young pigeons and turtle doves which hung from the baskets were presented for burnt-offerings. After that, each one, as he presented his gifts, repeated the solemn confession: 'I profess this day unto Jehovah thy God, that I am come unto the country that Jehovah swore unto our fathers for to give us' (Deut. xxvi. 3.). At these words, he took the basket from his shoulder, and the priest put his hands under it and waved it, the offerer continuing: 'A Syrian ready to perish was my father, and he went down into Egypt, and sojourned there with a few, and became there a nation—great, mighty, and populous.' Then, reciting in the words of inspiration the narrative of the Lord's marvellous dealings, he closed with the dedicatory language of verse 10: 'And, now, behold, I have brought the first fruits of the land which Thou, O Jehovah, hast given me.' So saying, he placed the basket at the side of the altar, cast himself on his face to worship, and departed."

CHAPTER VIII.

THE PSALMS IN THE ANCIENT SYNAGOGUE WORSHIP

§ I. *The Original Object of the Synagogue.*

IT will be necessary to consider the worship of the Synagogue as a whole in order to gain some clear idea of the part assigned here to the Psalms. For this purpose it will be well to gather, first of all, some of the evidence as to the *original* object of the meeting together in synagogues, which, as will be seen, was for the study of the Law, rather than for worship.

The earliest evidence is that of Philo ;—[1]

"Moses sat on the seventh day, surrounded by the priests, while all the people streamed together in order to be taught. For it was the custom in those far-off days—and especially on the Sabbath day—to philosophize; the leader discussed and taught concerning that which ought to be done and spoken, in order that the people might be encouraged in virtue, for the bettering of character and manner of life. Thus it has come about that now, too, the Jews devote themselves on the seventh day to the study of the philosophy inherited from their fore

[1] His date is approximately 20 B.C.—40 A.D.; his home was Alexandria. Most of the quotations from this writer here given are taken from M. Friedländer's *Synagoge und Kirche in ihren Anfängen*, pp. 61 ff.

fathers, and they dedicate this day to the study and contemplation of Nature. For what are the Jewish prayer-houses in the cities other than places of instruction in wisdom, caution, moderation, and righteousness, in piety and holiness, in short, in every virtue which recognises and accepts both human and divine goodness?"[1]

Again:

"On every Sabbath in every city there are numberless places of instruction opened for the teaching of wisdom, moderation, excellence, righteousness, and other virtues; in these the listeners sit in perfect order and absolute stillness, eagerly drinking in the most excellent doctrines. For here one of the most experienced puts forth the most perfect and most useful teaching by which human life can be adorned in the most beautiful way. For among the numerous precepts there are two of supreme importance; one deals with the Godhead, and is concerned with piety and holiness; the other deals with one's fellow-creatures, and is concerned with love and righteousness; each has many divisions dealing with conceptions so beautiful as to be beyond praise."[2]

Once more, in a fragment of Philo's preserved by Eusebius, we have the following:—

"Moses commanded the people to assemble themselves together in one place on the seventh day in order to listen with fear and reverence to the reading of the Law, so that each one might become conversant with the contents thereof. And in truth they meet together regularly, sitting side by side, the congregation usually silent, excepting where it is customary for them to join in in what is read.[3] One of the priests present,

[1] *Vita Mos.* ii. 168. [2] *De septen.* ii 282.

[3] This must refer to responses; the most important of these was the "Amen," *cp.* Deut. xxvii. 15, Tobit viii. 9, 1 Cor. xiv. 16; it is referred to in the Mishna, *e.g.*, *Berakhoth* viii. 8.

or one of the elders, reads to them the holy laws and explains each fully until the evening; thereupon they return home, enriched with the knowledge of the holy laws and making progress in piety. Does there exist a more striking institution than this one? Therefore, they have no need to go to the expounders of the laws in order to enquire concerning this and that; for by means of this institution they become learned in the Law, and do nothing that is contrary to it. And if thou shouldest ask any of them about the laws of their fathers, he would be able to give information regarding all of them with the greatest precision. Thus each one, whether husband, father, or master, is fully able to teach the Law to his wife, his children, or to his servants."[1]

These references are to the ordinary synagogues of the Jewish colonies in the Dispersion; Philo speaks in another place of the synagogues of the Essenes:

"For the seventh day is kept holy. On this day they rest from all work, and betake themselves to holy places, called synagogues, where they sit down in order, the younger ones behind the older, and listen with fitting demeanour. Thereupon one of them takes up one of the books and reads, while another, among the more experienced, steps forward and explains the difficult passages; for, according to the ancient method, these are for the most part interpreted symbolically, *i.e.* allegorically."[2]

Elsewhere Philo speaks of synagogues as being places for *prayer* (*In Flacc.* 6, 7; *Leg. ad Gaium* 20, 23, 43, 46; *Vita Mos.*, iii., 27), and in one passage he refers to "chants, hymns, and songs"[3] as being sung there.

[1] *Præp. evan.* viii. 7.

[2] *Quod omn. prob.* ., 458.

[3] *In Flacc.* 14 παιᾶνες, ὕμνοι, ᾠδαί.

The evidence of Josephus is as follows. In a decree of Cæsar Augustus, quoted by him, occurs this passage:

"Since the nation of the Jews hath been found grateful to the Roman people . . . it seemed good to me and to my counsellors, according to the sentence and oath of the people of Rome, that the Jews should have liberty to make use of their own customs, according to the law of their forefathers. . . . But if anyone be caught stealing their holy books, or their sacred money, whether it be out of the synagogue, or public school, he shall be deemed a sacrilegious person. . . ."

Elsewhere he speaks of the synagogue as a *Proseucha*, "Place of prayer"; he says it was "a large edifice, and capable of receiving a great number of people"; the reference is to the synagogue at Tiberias.[2] In another passage he speaks of Moses having commanded the people to assemble every Sabbath-day for the hearing of the Law: ". . . . permitting the people to leave off their other employments, and to assemble together for the hearing of the Law, and learning it exactly; and this not once or twice, or oftener, but every Sabbath."[3]

The evidence of Philo and Josephus is, thus, to the same effect; the synagogue was primarily a place for the study of, and instruction in, the Law; it was also a house of prayer, though in a less degree; Philo uses the name "house of prayer" (προσευχή) more often than "place of assembly" (συναγωγή); Josephus uses the

[1] *Antiq.* XVI., vi. 2 (Margoliouth's ed., 1906). [2] *Vita* § liv.
[3] *Contra Ap.* II. 17.

latter term several times, the former only once. On the other hand, Philo does once refer to singing in the synagogue.

We turn next to the New Testament; only those passages are referred to which may be thought to throw some light on the question of the nature of the service in the synagogue.

As a place of *teaching*, the synagogue is referred to in the following passages: Matth. iv. 23, ix. 35, xiii. 54; Mark i. 21, 22, vi. 2; Luke iv. 15, 31, 32, vi. 6, xiii. 10; John vi. 59, xviii. 20; Acts xvii. 2 ff., 17, xviii. 4, 19, 26, xix. 8. As a place of *preaching*, usually associated with teaching, the synagogue is referred to in: Matth. iv. 23, ix. 35; Mark i. 39; Luke iv. 44; Acts ix. 20, xiii. 5, 16 ff., xiv. 1, xv. 21. The *reading of the Scriptures* in the synagogue is spoken of in: Luke iv. 16-30 (the Prophetical books), Acts xiii. 14, 15 (the Law and the Prophets), xv. 21 (the Law), xvii. 10, 11 (studyiug the Scriptures). In only one passage is *Prayer* mentioned in connexion with the synagogue (Matth. vi. 5), but here it is implied that it was the regular practice there (*cp.* Acts iv. 24, the place where St. Peter and St. John met their followers evidently corresponded to the synagogue proper, *cp.* v. 31, "and when they had prayed, the place was shaken wherein they were gathered together").[1] Other passages show that the synagogue was by no means restricted to the purposes of worship in the wider sense. Cases of

[1] ἐν ᾧ συνηγμένοι.

healing, etc., are mentioned as taking place therein: Matth. iv. 23., ix. 35, xii. 9 ff.; Mark i. 23-28, iii. 1-6; Luke iv. 33-35, vi. 6-11, xiii. 10-17; it was also used for holding judicial enquiries and for carrying out the sentence of punishment, see Matth. x. 17, xxiii. 34; Mark xiii. 9; Luke xii. 11, xxi. 12. Once a reference is made to the *singing of psalms* (1 Cor. xiv. 26, "When ye come together, each one hath a psalm . . . "); although it is a Christian assembly which is spoken of here there can be no doubt that the first Christian congregations followed the procedure of the Synagogue in their form of service; the earliest Jewish-Christians worshipped in the synagogue (see Acts xxii. 19, xxvi. 11), and in the Temple (see Acts ii. 46, 47, iii. 1, v. 42, xxi. 26, xxii. 17, xxiv. 17, 18).

We come now to the evidence to be gained from post-biblical Jewish literature. There is every reason to believe that the tradition, according to which the Synagogue service was made to correspond as far as possible with that of the Temple[1] contains some truth. "The earliest elements of synagogal worship," says Prof. Blau, "were developed from the Temple service and the custom of sacrificial watches (*Ma'amad*), as well as from private and public worship, from psalms and prayers which were composed at different times for special occasions . . . . It took centuries before the order of prayer as found in the Babylonian

[1] The east end of the Synagogue is called the *Hêkal* ("Temple") or *Kôdesh* ("Sanctuary") even at the present day.

Talmud became established ; it was neither desired nor was it possible to give it a fixed and definite form."[1] The Rabbis taught that for the sacrifices of the altar was substituted the study of the law ; in the Midrash *Sifre* 80 *a* it is said : "Just as the service at the altar was called an *Aboda* (*i.e.* sacrificial service), so also is the study of the Law" ; and according to *Sifra* 80 *a*, prayer is equivalent to the offering of sacrifice.[2] In the Talmud, *Berakhoth* 24 *b* 26 *b*, it is taught that the daily prayers of the Synagogue have taken the place of the daily sacrifices in the Temple ; thus, the Morning Service corresponds to the morning offering, for which reason it may be said any time before mid-day ; the *Mincha*—or Afternoon Service—corresponds to the evening offering, for which reason it may be postponed until the evening ; while the Evening Service corresponds to the burning of the sacrifice, for which reason it may be said any time during the night.[3]

This illustrates what Bacher says,[4] that "As the place of public worship, the synagogue became the pivot of each community, just as the Sanctuary at Jerusalem had been the centre for the entire people. Ezek. xi. 16, *Yet will I be to them as a little sanctuary*, was rightly interpreted, therefore, to mean that in its

[1] Prof. Blau in the *Jewish Encycl.* viii. 137*ab;* see also Zunz, *Die Ritus des synagogalen Gottesdienstes*, pp. 1 ff. Josephus once (*Bell Jud.* VII., iii. 1) speaks of the synagogue at Antioch as τὸ ἱερόν "the Holy Place," which is otherwise only applied to the Temple.

[2] See Weber, *Jüdische Theologie*, pp. 39 f.

[3] Weber, *Op. cit.* p. 40.

[4] *Jewish Encycl.* xi. 623*a*.

dispersion Israel would retain the synagogue as a sanctuary in miniature in compensation for the loss of the Temple, and the community crystallized around the synagogue, the only possible organisation for the Jews of the Diaspora. Synagogal worship, therefore, however much it might vary in detail in different countries, was the most important visible expression of Judaism, and the chief means of uniting the Jews scattered throughout the world." As illustrating further how the thought of the Temple always lay behind that of the Synagogue, Dembitz refers to the prohibition in the Mishna[1] about using the Temple Mount as a thoroughfare, which has always been applied to the Synagogue; the prohibition is as follows: "One may not walk upon the Temple Mount with a stick, nor with shoes on, nor with a bag of money, nor with dust upon one's feet; nor must it be used as a short cut; as to spitting there, that is altogether forbidden."

§ II. *The Order of Service in the Ancient Synagogue.*

There existed in the Temple, apart from the offering of sacrifices, an elaborate liturgy, the central part of which was the singing of Psalms with the accompanying music; these have always occupied an important part in the liturgy of the Synagogue. "Those Psalms which are cast in the form of prayers and hymns soon took their place as hymns in the service of the sanctuary, even though they were not originally composed

[1] *Berakhoth* ix. 5.

for this purpose, and they were sung, especially on feast-days, in the synagogue, and in private gatherings. In its descriptions of Temple festivities the Book of Chronicles alludes to them, especially to the eighteen 'Hallelujah,' 'Hallel,' and 'Hodu' Psalms (Pss. cv-cvii., cxi-cxviii., cxxxv., cxxxvi., cxlvi-cl.) . . . Prophecy and Psalmody were gradually typified in two persons, Moses and David. . . . Even after the destruction of the Temple these united elements left their impress upon the Synagogue; the readings were devoted to the Law, and the discourses to the Prophets, while entire Psalms, or verses from them, were used as prayers."[1] Professor Blau says: "In the ritual of the Synagogue the Psalms retain their ancient position, at least as regards the text of the prayers; 'in the Sabbath and Festival discourses the wise man becomes the prophet, and the leader in prayer the psalmist.'"[2] The Psalms are represented in a further way in the liturgy of the Synagogue, viz., in the utterance of doxologies during public worship; to quote Prof. Blau again: "The adjuration 'Praise God' was probably addressed to the people of earlier times only in the flush of victory after deliverance from the dangers of war (Judg. v. 2. 9), but later, when a regular Temple cult had been instituted, it may have been uttered daily, so that it became a liturgical formula with which Divine worship was generally concluded (Ps. lxviii. 26, c 4,

[1] Zunz, *Synagogale Poesie des Mittelalters*, pp. 4. ff., quoted by Prof. Blau, *Op. cit.* viii. 132 *b*. [2] *Ibid.*

etc.). In Ps. cxxxv (*cp.* also cxviii. 2-4) Israelites, priests, Levites, and the pious are summoned by groups to 'Bless the Lord!' and it is noteworthy that this invitation is placed at the conclusion of the Psalm. The final verse: 'Blessed be the Lord out of Zion, which dwelleth at Jerusalem; praise ye the Lord,' constituted the benediction spoken by those who had been summoned. The benedictions that conclude the closing chapters of the five books of Psalms (xli., lxxii., lxxxix., cvi., cl.), all being in substance one and the same eulogy, may represent synagogal formulas from the time of the Temple, which the people intoned after completing the singing of the several books. Occasionally, however, the people concluded with a simple 'Amen' (*cp.* the Psalms quoted and 1 Chron. xvi. 36). It may also be assumed that such benedictions were not reserved for public worship exclusively, but were also pronounced in private: 'I will bless the Lord at all times; his praise shall continually be in my mouth' (Ps. xxxiv. 2, *cp.* cxv. 18, cxlv. 2). Mention is made of supplications at 'evening and morning, and at noon' (Ps. lv. 17), and of praise offered seven times a day (Ps. cxix. 164), while in another passage only praise rendered in the morning is mentioned. The origin of this liturgical usage was the custom, on joyful occasions, of praising God for His goodness."[1]

Thus the reading of Scripture, the Prayers, and the Psalms (not necessarily in this order) formed, from the

[1] *Op. cit.* viii. 134 *b.*

beginning, the component parts of the worship of the Synagogue. Schürer is, therefore, right (excepting for one important omission) when he sums up what is said about the worship of the Synagogue in the Mishna (*Megilla* iv. 3): "The chief parts were, according to the Mishna, the recitation of the *Shema'*,[1] Prayer, the reading of the *Torah*, the reading of the Prophets, the Blessing of the priest. To these were added the translation[2] of the portions of Scripture read, which is assumed in the Mishna, and the explanation of what had been read by an edifying discourse.[3] To this should be added the praise portion of the service, which, as we have seen, occupied an important place in the worship of the Synagogue.

Scattered about in various Jewish writings there are a number of details regarding the different parts of Synagogue-worship; some of these throw sidelights upon the subject under discussion, others have an interest of their own. A small selection of these may be appropriately added here.

In the Mishna (*Nedarim* v. 5) certain things are enumerated which are the property of a community; among these are reckoned, "the Synagogue (*Beth ha-Keneseth*) the ark, and the books"; by the "books"

[1] *I.e.* Deut. vi. 4-9, xi. 13-21; Num. xv. 37-41; and certain "Benedictions" attached to it.

[2] Aramaic had displaced Hebrew as the vernacular before the Hasmonean period, the middle of the 2nd cen. B.C.

[3] *The Jewish People in the time of Jesus Christ* (Engl. Transl.), Div. II., Vol. II., p. 76.

are meant primarily, the rolls of the Law; it was (and is) usual to have more than one copy of this; besides these, there was the roll containing the prophetical books; it must also be assumed that other rolls, containing books of the *Hagiographa,* were also included. In some parts of the East, Nehardea in Babylonia is specially mentioned, it was customary to read portions from the *Hagiographa,* at the Sabbath afternoon service,[1] as well as from the Law and the Prophets. Some books of the *Hagiographa* have been used on special occasions for many ages, the *Megilloth* (*Song of Songs, Ruth, Lamentations, Ecclesiastes, Esther*), for example, of which *Esther* is read right through at the Feast of Purim,[2] and *Lamentations* is read on the ninth of Ab,[3] the fast kept in memory of the destruction of Jerusalem. How far the books of the *Hagiographa* were studied, in early days, in the way in which the rest of the Scriptures were is uncertain; there is a Targum to the *Psalms* and *Job,* which apparently belong together; this must, in its origin, be ancient, for in it Rome and Constantinople are mentioned as the two capitals of the Roman Empire, thus presupposing a date of compilation at the latest before the fall of Rome in 476 A.D. Important in this connexion is Luke xxiv. 44: "These are my words which I spake unto you, while I was yet with you, how that all things

[1] Babylonian Talmud, *Shabbath* 116 *a b*; whether this was done in the West cannot be said, there is no evidence for it.

[2] Babylonian Talmud, *Megilla* 70 *a*.

[3] *Massechet Sopherim* xviii. 4.

must needs be fulfilled, which are written in the Law of Moses, and the Prophets, and the Psalms, concerning me" (*cp.* Acts i. 20, ii. 25-28, 34, 35; iv. 25, 26), which implies a study of the Psalms apart from their use in the service of praise; it is, therefore, possible that some of the psalms were at one time read and commented upon in the Synagogue.

In the Talmudic tractate *Sopherim*[1] a number of particulars are given about the use of the Psalms in the Early Synagogue; here we are often told about what psalms were used on special occasions, and why they were chosen. For example Ps. vii. was one of those sung at the Feast of *Purim* because it speaks of vengeance on the adversary,[2] see verses 6, 11-16, *cp.* Esth. ix. 13 ff.; on the other hand, in the Midrash *Tehillim* (*in loc.*) "Cush the Benjamite," mentioned in the title of this psalm, is said to refer to Saul. Ps. xxx. was sung on the Feast of Dedication (*Channukah*, called also "The Feast of Maccabees"),[3] as its title says; it was transferred from the Temple, after the destruction, to the Synagogue.[4] Another example of

[1] The text, with notes has been published by Joel Müller (Leipzig 1878); this tractate belongs, according by Zunz (*Die gottesdienstlichen Vorträge der Juden*, p. 101, 2nd ed.) to the period of the *Geonim*, which began in 589 A.D., and extended to the eleventh century.

[2] *Sopherim* xviii 2.

[3] See 1 Macc. iv. 59, 2 Macc. i. 18; in the Talmud it is usually called the "Feast of Illumination" (*cp.* Josephus, *Antiq.* XII., vii. 7, where it is called "The Feast of Lights, Φῶτα), on account of the lamps lighted on each day of the feast, eight on the first day, and one less on each succeeding day.

[4] *Sopherim* xviii. 2.

earlier usage, which is preserved in this tractate, is in regard to the special psalm (xlvii.) sung at the festival of the New Year;[1] this psalm was evidently chosen on account of v. 5 (in Heb. v. 6): "God is gone up with a shout, the Lord with the sound of the trumphet" (*shôphar*); the blowing of the ram's-horn, or "*shôphar*," is one of the characteristic ceremonies of this festival; but the special psalm for this festival is elsewhere given as lxxxi.,[2] chosen because of the reference to the "*shôphar*" in v. 3 (Hebr. v. 4). Again, two special psalms are mentioned for the festival of the New Moon, Ps. xcviii. on account of the reference in v. 6 to the *shôphar*, which, according to Num. x. 10, was blown on the New Moons, and Ps. civ.,[3] because of verses 1, 2; in later times, the latter of these two alone became the proper psalm for this festival. The special psalm for the Feast of Tabernacles is given as lxxvi.[4]; Ps. cxviii. 25 to the end, which appears originally to have been a separate psalm, was also proper to this festival.[5] Ps. cxxx. is explained in reference to the Day of Atonement.[6] We are told, further, and the fact is interesting, that the "Hallelujah"-psalms were known by heart by the people,[7] these Psalms are civ.-cvi., cxi.-cxiii., cxv.-cxvii., cxxxv., cxlvi.-cl.; in some

[1] *Ibid.* xix. 2. [2] *Rosh Hashshana* 30 *b*, see also Midrash *Tehillim* on this psalm. [3] *Sopherim* xvii. 11. [4] *Ibid.* xix. 2.

[5] Mishna, *Sukkah* iv. 3., and see Müller's note in his edition of *Sopherim*, p. 288. [6] *Sopherim* xix. 2.

[7] See Müller's note in his edition of *Sopherim*, p. 263.

[8] *Jewish Encycl.* vi. 179 *a*.

of these psalms, as Dembitz points out,[8] "this opening phrase is developed in the words which follow it; in others, such as cxi., cxii., it does not run naturally in the psalm, and seems to have been prefixed by the authorities of the Temple to fit the psalm into public worship." According to Rab,[1] the name of the whole Psalter should be called "Hallelujah," because this word contains both the name of God (*Jah*, *cp.* Ps. lxviii. 4) and its glorification (*Hallelu*—"Praise ye").[2] It is said (*cp. Sopherim* xvi. 11, 12) that the "Hallelujah" was uttered one hundred and twenty-three times by the people; the reference is to the singing of the *Hallel*, for, as we are told in the Talmud (*Sukkah* 38 *b*), the people responded with "Hallelujah" after each verse-division of the *Hallel*. Müller, in his note on this passage in *Sopherim*, says that if one counts up the verse-divisions in the *Hallel* according to its poetical structure, it will be seen that these number exactly one hundred and twenty-three.[3] It was a later and fanciful idea, which held that this number was chosen because it corresponded with the years of Aaron's life (see Num. xxxiii. 39). As in the Temple, so in the Synagogue the *Hallel* has always occupied a position of peculiar importance, and the Temple usage of singing this at the great festivals has been followed in the Synagogue.

[1] *I.e.* Rabbi Abba Arika; he lived early in the 3 cen. A.D.

[2] Midrash *Tehillim* i. 1.

[3] The frequent utterance of "Hallelujah" in early forms of Christian worship, was obviously borrowed from this Jewish usage.

From what has been said, therefore, the order of worship in the ancient Synagogue may, with much probability, be described as follows; some elements in the following description have not been touched upon in what has been said above, because our main object has been to try and ascertain the place of the Psalms in the Synagogue-worship; but there is evidence, which will be briefly indicated in foot-notes, to show that these other elements may with practical certainty be regarded as having constituted essential parts of the earliest form of Synagogue-worship.

1. The offering-up of Prayer by a recognised official minister;[1] we are definitely told that the prayer called *'Ahabah Rabbah*[2] ("Great Love") was said before the reading from the Law.[3]

2. The reading of passages from the Law,[4] such

[1] In the Midrash *Bereshith Rabba*, in the comment on Genesis xviii. 23, mention is made of one of the ministers, who stood before the Ark in order to offer up prayer. The technical name for this official was *Shiliach Zibbor*, called later *Chazzan*, see Zunz, *Op. cit*. p. 393.

[2] A Benediction founded originally, it is supposed, on Jer. xxxi. 3 (" . . . Yea, I have loved thee with an everlasting love; therefore with loving-kindnesses have I drawn thee"); it was a thanksgiving for God's love in having given the revelation of the Torah to Israel.

[3] Mishna, *Middoth* v. i.

[4] This is based on ancient custom, possibly on Deut. xxxi. 12., "Assemble the people . . . . that they may hear, and that they may learn, and fear the Lord your God, and observe to do all the words of this law." In later times the lesson from the Law was technically known as the *Parashah* ("Section"); this was read on Sabbaths, and the first part of it on the following second and fifth days of the week at Morning Prayer.

as the *Shema*[1] and the Ten Commandments. These were read in Hebrew, and as each verse was read it was translated into the vernacular (Aramaic) by the *Methurgeman*, or officially appointed translator.

3. The offering up of Prayer, namely the *Tephilla* ("Prayer") or *Shemoneh 'Esreh* ("Eighteen Benedictions.")[2]
4. The reading of a passage from the Prophetical books.[3]
5. An exhortation based on what had been read.[4]
6. The offering of Praise; it is probable that this was introduced by the singing, or recitation of the *Trisagion* ("Holy, holy, holy, is the Lord of hosts, the whole earth is full of his glory," Is. vi. 3.), and the *Baruk Kebôd 'Adonai* ("Blessed be the glory of the Lord from his

[1] As a constituent element in Synagogue-worship this is very ancient; it must have been in use before the beginning of the Christian Era at the latest, as Rabbi Gamaliel (end of first century, A.D.) regards it as a fixed element in worship in deciding that it can be recited till dawn (Mishna, *Berakhoth* i. 1.)

[2] For the great antiquity of this prayer, especially its earliest portions, see Zunz, *Op. cit.* pp. 380 ff. Regarding prayer in the Service see also the Mishna, *Berakhoth* v. 5, and *Rosh Hashshana* iv. 9.

[3] In later days this portion of Scripture was technically known as the *Haphtarah* ("Conclusion"). This was translated by the *Methurgeman* after every three verses; both in regard to this and to the lesson from the Pentateuch, the sense of the passage was taken into consideration, so that often more or less than one verse from the Law, and more or less than three verses from the Prophets, might be read before being translated.

[4] *Cp.* Acts xiii. 15, xiv. 1.

place," Ezek. iii. 12); this was uttered both in Hebrew at Aramaic.[1] After this it is probable that the psalm for the day was sung. Excepting for the final Blessing this concluded the service. The custom of finishing the daily prayers with praise to God is very ancient.[2]

7. The "Aaronic Blessing," with the "Amen" by the people (see Num. vi. 24 ff.).

With what has been said *cp.* Matth. iv. 23, ix. 35, Mark i. 29, Luke iv. 17 ff., 44, John xviii. 20, Acts xiii. 5, 14, 15, xiv. 1, 2 Cor. iii. 14, 15.

As Müller truly says: "A similar order of worship was in vogue in the Church during the earliest centuries, where the reading from the Old Testament was followed by a reading from the Gospels, the praise portion proper coming at the end of the service."[3] In this connexion the following from the *Peregrinatio Etheriae*[4] is of interest; it is taken from the Sunday offices, *Vigil:* "And when the people have entered, one of *the priests says a psalm to which all respond, and afterwards prayer is made;* then one of the deacons says *a psalm, and prayer is again made;* a *third psalm* is recited by one of the clergy, *prayer is*

[1] See Müller's notes on *Sopherim*, pp. 226 f.

[2] See Müller, *Op. cit.* p. 226, and *cp.* the prayer of Hezekiah (Is. xxxvii. 15-20), which is preceded and concluded with praise to God.

[3] *Op. cit.* p. 227.

[4] Reprinted, from Duchesne's *Christian Worship*, by the Society for Promoting Christian Knowledge, under the title, "Holy Week in Jerusalem in the fourth century," p. 550.

made for the third time, and there is a commemoration for all . . . . After the reading of the Gospel the Bishop goes out, and is accompanied to the Cross by all the people with hymns, there again *a psalm is said and prayer is made*, after which he blesses the faithful, and the Dismissal takes place."

Here praise, followed by prayer, occurs at the beginning as well as at the end of the service, but, broadly speaking, the component parts of the service are: Praise and Prayer, then the central Prayer portion (the "commemoration of all"), after that the reading of Scripture, concluding with Praise and Prayer; then the final Blessing. This corresponds in the main outline with the earliest form of Synagogue Worship.[1]

§ III. *The Music of the Ancient Synagogue.*

With regard to the *Music of the Synagogue* the following words from Mr. F. L. Cohen's able article on "Music" in the *Jewish Encyclopædia*[2] are worth quoting: "The earliest synagogal music was founded upon the same system and method as prevailed in the orchestra of the Temple itself. Joshua Ben Hananiah, who had served in the sanctuary as a member of the Levitical choir,[3] told how the choristers went in a body to

[1] Most of the "Korah" psalms end with praise, viz., xlii. 2, xliii. 5 [not xliv], xlv. 17, xlvi. 11, xlvii. 9, lviii. 14 [not xlix], lxxxiv. 11, 12 [not lxxxv.], [not lxxxvii], [not lxxxviii]; this very possibly points to a tendency to conclude prayer with praise; *cp.* Ps. vii. 17.

[2] ix. 120 *a*.

[3] Babylonian Talmud, *'Arakhin* 11 *b*.

the Synagogue from the orchestra by the altar,[1] and so participated in both services." It is also important to note that when, later on, after the destruction of the Temple, instrumental music was no more heard in Jewish worship, the *method of singing* was not thereby altered; "as the part of the instruments in the Temple musical *ensemble* was purely that of accompaniment, and the voices could have given an adequate rendition without accompaniment, the absence of instruments from the Synagogue in no way modified the system of the song itself." It follows, therefore, that although the old Synagogue music that has come down to us is post-Christian, it is not for that reason not ancient. The earliest Synagogue choir consisted of at the least twelve Levites, in addition to boys' voices; the Mishna[3] tells us, further, that the *kinnor* was played by nine of the singers, the *nebel* by two, and the cymbals by one; the flute was only played on holy days.[4] It is, thus, clear that originally the Psalms were *sung*, and not said, in the Synagogue; this is true of the Jerusalem synagogues, and therefore probably also of the Palestinian synagogues generally; with regard to those of the Dispersion the evidence is less clear, but see the reference to Philo above, p. 131. Rabbi Hirsch[5] says:

[1] The singers stood at the east end of the bronze altar of the burnt-offering (see 2 Chron. v. 12).

[2] *'Arakhin* 13 *b*. [3] *'Arakhin* ii. 3-5.

[4] Mishna, *'Arakhin* ii. 3. [5] *Jewish Encycl*. x. 247 *b*.

"In the synagogues the Psalms were chanted antiphonally, the congregation often repeating after every verse chanted by the precentor the first verse of the psalm in question. 'Hallelujah' was the word with which the congregation was invited to take part in this chanting. Hence it originally prefaced the psalms, not as in the Massoretic text, coming at the end. At the conclusion of the psalms, the *makre*, or 'precentor' added a doxology ending with 'And say ye Amen,' whereupon the congregation replied 'Amen, Amen' (*Monatschrift* 1872, p. 481)."

"The contemporaneous fashion of the outer world has ever found its echo within the walls of the synagogue, so that in the superstructure added by successive generations of transmitting singers, there are always discernible points of comparison, even of contact, with the style and structure of each successive era in the musical history of other religious communions. Attention has frequently been drawn to the resemblances in manner, and even in some points of detail, between the chants of the *muezzin* and of the reader of the Koran with much of the *chazzanut*,[1] not alone of the Sephardim, who passed so many centuries in Arab lands, but also of the Ashkenazim, equally long located far away in northern Europe. The intonations of the Sephardim even more intimately recall the plain-song of the Mozarabian Christians, which flourished in their

[1] *I.e.* The traditional mode of intonation of the *Chazzan*, the Synagogue official who conducted the musical and other portions of the service, see *Sopherim* x. 7, and, for many other details of the office, Zunz, *Synagogale Poesie des Mittelalters*, pp. 144 ff.

proximity until the thirteenth century. Their chants and other set melodies largely consist of very short phrases, oft repeated, just as Perso-Arab melody so often does; and their congregational airs usually preserve a Morisco or other Peninsular character."[1] There can be little doubt that, in some cases, very ancient traditional musical pieces are embodied in the music of the modern Synagogue; such pieces have, no doubt, tended to become modified in the course of centuries, but, even in their primitive form, it is very questionable whether they are pre-Christian. The *data* as to early song in general given in the introductory chapter permit us to form some idea of what the original melodies of the Temple, and therefore of the ancient Synagogue, must have been, but of their actual *form* we cannot claim to know anything; that is to say, we cannot take even the simplest synagogal melody of the present day and say that in its present form it was used in the ancient synagogue. The introduction of *Piyyutim*[2] were certainly, in part, responsible for this, because the singing of these required more elaborate melodies than had hitherto obtained; and, as we shall see, they drove the Psalms into a subordinate position in the service. It followed, therefore, that many of the ancient melodies were lost irretrievably. But though we have lost the actual melodies of ancient synagogal worship, there is no sort of doubt as to the fact that

[1] *Jewish Encycl.* ix. 121 *b*.

[2] On these, see the next two chapters.

a fairly elaborate use of music existed in the Synagogue, even in pre-Christian times. We have already seen that the Levitical choir came direct to the synagogue after its duties in the Temple had been fulfilled. Mr. F. L. Cohen, in his excellent article on "Music" in the *Jewish Encycl.*, already quoted, gives further evidence as to this during the early Christian centuries, and there is no reason to doubt that this reflects earlier usage. "The dispersal of the Temple singers," he says, "and the cessation of the performances of the musicians in the sanctuary influenced but slightly the synagogal cantillation, since the desire of many authorities that song should be abstained from in lasting mourning for fallen Zion, was never generally heeded when it became a question of song in worship. Indeed, from the earlier centuries there had been an evident desire to enhance the importance of the singing in the synagogal ritual. The officiant was required to have a pleasant voice and a clear enunciation, and the voluntary assistance of good vocalists was regarded as meritorious . . . The Psalms were chanted originally in a responsive antiphony; but soon the antiphony developed into a general unison . . ."[1]

For many ancient synagogal melodies given in full, see De Sola, *The Ancient Melodies of the Spanish and Portuguese Jews* (1857).

[1] Copious references to original authorities are given in support of all the statements made.

CHAPTER IX.

THE PSALMS IN THE MODERN SYNAGOGUE.

SOME insight into the use of the Psalms in the modern Synagogue will be found of interest from several points of view. To begin with, it is clearly a question of interest to know the position which the Psalms now occupy in public worship among those people whose forefathers first gave them to the world. Although the Church has made the Psalms peculiarly her own—her use of them is greater than has ever been the case in the Jewish Church—and although she has, generally speaking, been more thorough in her recognition and appreciation of their unrivalled beauty, and of the intense religious feeling which permeates them, nevertheless the Psalms are the product of the Jewish Church, a possession which that Church preserved and cherished long before the Christian era. It is, therefore, we repeat, a matter of interest to see what use is made of the Psalms in the Jewish Liturgy of to-day. Then, again, this question is not without importance for the study of the history of Synagogue-worship generally. Towards the end of the eighteenth century a revivification took place in the liturgical worship of the Synagogue, which for many centuries previously had been suffering grievous decay; an intense desire arose to reform the Liturgy. It is interesting to note, by the way, that in one respect, at least, the deadness in public worship from which the Synagogue suffered resembled a similar deadness which characterized the worship of the Church of England at one time; instead of making the use of the Psalms one of the most prominent elements in the service, as had been done in the early Synagogue, following herein the worship of the Temple, the recitation of numberless *Piyyutim*[1] came into vogue, with the result that the Psalms were pushed into quite a subordinate position. This procedure is strongly reminiscent of the time when Tate and Brady's "New Version of the Psalms was used in place of the Psalter. At the same time, the analogy only holds good in part, for it is necessary to emphasize the fact that in the Synagogue the use of the officially selected psalms of the Liturgy was never discontinued; these psalms were overweighted, and pushed into a position of inferiority, by the *Piyyutim.* The latter came to occupy the central place of importance, while the psalms were hurriedly recited, as though an insignificant, albeit a necessary, part of the service.

[1] *I.e.* Poems, of much later times, many of which were quite inferior productions; see further on this subject below, pp. 179 ff.

When the reform of the Liturgy took place it was in three directions, mainly, viz.: in the introduction of new elements, in alterations of the prevailing use, and in the re-introduction of ancient and genuine liturgical forms;[1] but, of these three, the last constituted by far the most important factor. So that in studying the use of the Psalms in the modern Jewish Liturgy we shall, in reality, be gaining, in this particular at all events, some insight into the early custom of the Synagogue.

The two great bodies into which orthodox Jews are divided, the Ashkenazim and the Sephardim, have each their own Liturgy, and these differ in some respects as to the psalms used on different occasions. It will, therefore, be necessary to indicate where they differ in important places; but there will be no need to point out every variation between the two uses.

§ I. *The Psalms in the Daily Services.*

There are three daily services in the Synagogue-worship, viz. *Shacharith* (Morning Prayer), *Minchah* (Afternoon Prayer), *Maarib* (Evening Prayer). To deal with the *Morning Service* first. On entering the synagogue each worshipper says, privately, a number of verses taken from different psalms, beginning with: "As for me, in the abundance of Thy loving-kindness will I come into Thy house; I will worship

[1] Zunz lays much stress on this; see the many details he gives to prove his statements in *Die gottesdienstlichen Vorträge der Juden*, pp. 490 ff.

towards Thy holy temple in the fear of Thee" (Psalm v. 7).

In connexion with some congregations there exists what is known as a *Chevrah Tehillim*, *i.e.* a society the members of which make a point of reading the Psalms before the daily Morning Service. In this way they read through the whole Psalter once a week. Although this is done in the synagogue the institution is a private and voluntary one; and the saying of psalms by the members of a *Chevrah Tehillim* has nothing to do with the official service of the synagogue.

After a hymn of praise, and readings from the Mishna and the Old Testament, which include passages from the Psalms, Psalm c. is said, "Shout for joy unto the Lord, all ye lands"; this is an invitation, as it were, to all peoples to join in worshipping the One God. There follow then, after some words of praise, to which the preceding psalm has given the keynote, Psalms cxlv.-cl., the last verse of the last psalm being repeated. These are preceded by the versicles: "Happy are they that dwell in Thy house, they will be ever praising Thee. Happy is the people that is in such a case; happy is the people whose God is the Lord" (Psalms lxxxiv. 4, cxliv. 15). These versicles are always used in introducing the recitation of Psalm cxlv. In the Babylonian Talmud, *Berakhoth* 45 *a*, Psalm xxxiv. 3 (4 in Hebrew) is explained as referring to the manner in which the Psalms should be sung, namely, first a blessing ("O magnify the Lord with me"), and then the praise ("And let us exalt His name together").[1] This Psalm (cxlv.) is said no less than three times during Morning Service. The following words from *Berakhoth* 4 *b* are of interest in this connexion: "He who says Psalm cxlv. three times daily may rest assured that he will inherit the life eternal." The Talmud suggests as a reason for this that the psalm in question teaches the universal providence of God, which is set forth in such verses as 15, 16, "The eyes of all wait upon Thee, and Thou givest them their meat in due season. Thou openest Thine hand, and satisfiest the desire of every living thing;" the psalm is regarded in the light of a prayer for all flesh, and the material blessings asked for are an earnest of the far greater spirtual blessings to be enjoyed hereafter. Further, when in this service, the prayer called the *Amidah* (="Standing," because it is said standing) is said, it is prefaced by the versicles: "O Lord, open Thou our lips, and our mouth shall show forth Thy praise" (Psalm li. 15). According to the Talmud (*Berakhoth* 4 *b*), the *Amidah* should conclude with, "Let the words of my mouth and the meditation of my heart, be acceptable in Thy sight, O Lord, my Rock, and my Redeemer" (Psalm xix. 14). This was evidently the ancient usage, and it seems a pity that the modern practice has deviated from this by adding instead the words from Job xxv. 2, "He

[1] See Müller's note in his edition of *Sopherim*, p. 290.

maketh peace in His high places," for nothing could be more appropriate than Psalm xix. 14 as a conclusion to the *Amidah.* Later on in the service, Psalm vi. is said, ("O Lord, rebuke me not in Thine anger"). On Mondays and Thursdays, the two week-days on which the Law is read, Psalm xxiv. is said after the reading; and when the *Sepher* (*i.e.* the "Scroll" of the Law) has been replaced in the Ark, Psalms cxlv., xx., are said.[1] They are preceded by the versicles quoted above in connexion with Psalm cxlv. It is not until towards the end of the service that the special psalm for the day is sung;[2] this, with the exception of the reading of the Law on Mondays and Thursdays, is the only part of the daily Morning Prayer that varies.[3] The daily special psalms are: On the first day of the week, Psalm xxiv.; on the second, Psalm xlviii.; on the third, Psalm lxxxii.; on the fourth, Psalm xciv.; on the fifth, Psalm lxxxi.; on the sixth, Psalm xciii.; and on the Sabbath, Psalm xcii. The psalm for the day is always prefaced by the words: "This is the—— day of the week, on which the Levites in the Temple used to say psalm —." According to the Mishna (see above, pp. 117 ff.), the psalm for the day was always *said;* this is also stated in the *Gemara*, the words used being *amar* and *dabar* respectively, both of

[1] These are also said every day whether the Law is read or not.

[2] Custom varies, however, as to the precise place in the service at which this is sung.

[3] Sabbaths, Festivals, and Fasts are, of course, excepted.

which are only used in reference to *saying*, not to singing; but it must be added that, in spite of this, there is justification for the statement of Mr. Box (*Encycl. Bibl.*, col. 4955) that "the choir of Levites, to the accompaniment of musical instruments,[1] *sang* the psalm of the day"; for at the close of each of the three sections into which the psalm of the day was always divided, the priests blew three blasts on the silver trumpets. Now the *saying* of a psalm would not be in keeping with these interludes of trumpet-blowing, the mention of which rather implies that the psalm was sung; and besides this, the psalm of the day is always sung in the modern Synagogue;[2] and when it is remembered that emphasis is laid on the fact that the use of the special daily psalm in the Synagogue has been taken over from the Temple-worship, it is right to assume that the mode of rendering it is likewise based on the usage of the Temple. After the special psalm for the day, Psalm lxxxiii. ("O God, keep not Thou silence") is added, though there are some exceptions to this; during part of the year, Psalm xxvii. is also said daily at Morning Prayer after Psalm lxxxiii.

In the Sephardic Ritual the psalms for this service are somewhat different; they are: xxx., ciii., xix., cxlv.-cl., xxv., xx., lxxxvi. (the last two are omitted on

[1] This is not specifically stated in the Mishna passage in *Tamid*, nor in the *Gemara* to it.

[2] In spite of the fact that in the Rubric in the Jewish Prayer Book the psalm is spoken of as being said.

the days when no "supplicatory prayers" are said); the special psalm for the day is the same as in the Ashkenazic Ritual.

The daily *Afternoon Service* is a shortened form of Morning Prayer; only three psalms figure here, cxlv., xxiv. (this psalm is, however, only said at this service on Saturdays and on Fast days, when the Law has to be read), and vi.; but the Sephardic Jews say Psalms lxxxiv., cxlv., xxv., lxvii during this service. At the daily *Evening Service* Psalm cxxxiv.[1] is said, according to both Rituals, but in the Sephardic Psalm cxxi. is also said. Among the Ashkenazic Jews, however, if Evening Prayer is said after night-fall the prescribed Psalms are xxiv., viii., xxix. The Ritual of these latter has also special psalms which are said at this service on the "Days of Omer";[2] they are xxv. xxxii., xxxviii., li., lxxxvi., on the first five days of the week respectively.

§ II. *The Psalms in the Sabbath Services.*

Among the Ashkenazic Jews there are, strictly

[1] This psalm is omitted when the Evening Service is said immediately after Mincha, which is often the case.

[2] *I.e.*, the days between the first day of Passover (eve of 15 Nisan) and Pentecost; the "counting of the Omer" is still practised (see Lev. xxiii. 10, 11), but the bringing of the Omer has ceased since the destruction of the Temple. "Omer" means "sheaf," though the early Rabbis interpreted it in the sense of a "measure" (*cp.* Exodus xvi. 36). In the Synagogue the bringing of the Omer is stated to be the repayment to the Almighty for having given the Israelites manna in the wilderness.

speaking, six Sabbath Services, but these are not all separated from each other.[1] During the service for the *Inauguration of the Sabbath*, Psalms xcv.-xcix, xxix., xcii. (this is the special psalm for the day), xciii. are sung.[2] The Sephardic Jews at their service on the *Eve of the Sabbath*, which corresponds to that just mentioned, sing Psalms xxix., xcii., xciii., xxiii. At *Morning Service*, according to the Ashkenazic Ritual, the ordinary week-day psalms for the corresponding service are said, viz., c., cxlv.-cl., and, in addition to these, Psalms xix., xxxiv., xc., xci.,[3] cxxxv., cxxxvi., xxxiii., xcii., xciii.; further, after the reading of the Law, Psalm xxix. or xxiv. is used. Most of these, but not all, are also found in the Sephardic Ritual, viz., Psalms xxxiii., xxxiv., xc., xci., xcviii., cxxi.-cxxiv., cxxxv., cxxxvi., xcii., xciii., cxlv. Among the Sephardic, as well as the Ashkenazic Jews, there is, after the Morning Service, what is called the *Additional Service for Sabbaths*[4] and Festivals, this is called *Musaf*.[5] During this service the extract from the Mishnic tractate *Tamid* is read which contains the passage

[1] *Cp.* the modern practice in the Church of combining the Litany with Morning Prayer.

[2] Regarding the singing, or saying of the Psalms, see below, § V.

[3] Whenever Psalm xci. is said, the last verse is invariably repeated.

[4] This service is also used, with slight variations, at Festivals and New Moons, and on the Day of Atonement.

[5] The *Musaf* Services take the place of the additional sacrifices brought on festive occasions, as commanded in the Law, see Numbers xxviii., xxix.

enumerating the special daily psalms which the Levites used to sing in the Temple. The only psalm used at this service is xcii., which is sung at the conclusion, after the "Unity Hymn for the Sabbath Day."[1] At the *Afternoon Service for Sabbaths*, Psalm xcii. is sung[2] while the vestments are being placed upon the scroll of the Law, prior to its being put back into the Ark; the psalms which are then said are the same as those used at the Morning Service after the reading of the Law. In the Sephardic Ritual, in addition to the ordinary week-day psalms for this service, Psalm cxi. is also said. At this Afternoon Service, from the first Sabbath after *Simcath Torah* ("The Rejoicing of the Law") until the Sabbath before Passover, Psalms civ., cxx.-cxxxiv., are said.

The *Evening Service* begins with two special Psalms, cxliv., lxvii., which are sung to a melody used by all Ashkenazic Congregations. Finally, there is the *Service for the Conclusion of the Sabbath*, at which Psalms cxliv., lxvii., are sung. These are chanted by the congregation before the ordinary Evening Service. The Sephardim also say privately, before this concluding service begins, Psalms cxviii.-cxxxiv., xvi., lxxv. In the Ashkenazic Ritual the service closes with Psalm cxxviii. But immediately

[1] This hymn is not recited by all Congregations.

[2] There is a lively traditional melody to which this psalm is sung common to all Ashkenazic and Polish Congregations.

after this service, forming in reality one with it, the *Habdala*[1] Service is said; this is introduced by various quotations from the Psalms, but no complete psalms are used. Besides what has been said, there is a special extra psalm for every Sabbath according to the lesson of the *Sedrah*.[2]

§ III. *The Psalms in the Festival Services.*

As the Ashkenazic and Sephardic Rituals differ somewhat in the selection of the psalms used during the Festivals, it will be best to take each separately, beginning with the former.

There are certain features, as regards the use of the psalms, which are alike at all the greater Festivals; thus, at the *Afternoon Service for the Eve* of a Festival, the versicles: "Happy are they that dwell in Thy house . . ." (Psalm lxxxiv. 4); "Happy is the people . . ." (Psalm cxliv. 15),[3] followed by Psalm cxlv., which belongs to the introductory part of the services, is common to all Festivals.[4] At the *Afternoon Service* of every Festival (if it does not fall on the Sabbath) Psalm xxiv. is read when the Roll of the Law is being returned to

[1] *I.e.*, "Separation"; the service has for its purpose the emphasizing of the difference between the Sabbath and ordinary days from which it is *separated.*

[2] The *Sedrah* ("Order") is the special portion of the Law read at Sabbath Morning Service.

[3] See § I. above.

[4] This is, of course, the ordinary Afternoon Service without "Supplication."

the Ark. Again, at the Morning Service of all the greater Festivals the passage from *Tamid* vii., enumerating the special psalms for each week-day as sung in the Temple, is read. Further, the Hallel (Psalms cxiii.-cxviii.)[1] is said prior to the reading from the Law; but the last Psalm (cxviii.) is said thus: the first four verses are chanted by the reader, the congregation responding with the first verse at the end of each of these four verses; up to verse 21 the psalm is recited in the ordinary way (*i.e.*, alternately by the reader and the congregation, but there is no fixed custom for this; it is sometimes said silently, see § V. below); verses 21-24 inclusive are each repeated; each clause of verse 25 is chanted first by the reader, and then by the congregation; verses 26-29 are each repeated. The Hallel is used at all the Festivals, excepting that of New Year; it is not said at this Festival because there is no miracle connected with the history of Israel which is commemorated by this day; moreover, it is the "Day of Judgement,"[2] and therefore not a day on which God's praises, which are contained in the Hallel, should be recited.[3] Another feature, as far

[1] On the last six days of Passover, and on New Moon Festivals, Psalms cxv. and cxvi. are omitted.

[2] In the Mishna (*Rosh Hashshana* i. 2) it is taught that on New Year's Day all the inhabitants of the world pass before the Lord for judgement as the sheep before a shepherd (*cp.* Matthew xxv. 31 ff.).

[3] Mr. I. Abrahams has, in his *Festival Studies*, an excellent chapter (xxii.) on the use of the Hallel at Festivals.

as the psalms are concerned, common to all the great Festivals, is that at the Evening Service Psalms xcii., xciii., are said; moreover, at the Morning Service for Festivals after the "Hymn of Glory" (this hymn contains many verses from the Psalms) has been sung, 1 Chronicles xvi. 8-36 is read, and this is followed by Psalms xix., xxxiv., xc., xci., cxxxv., cxxxvi., xxxiii., xcii., xciii., cxlv.-cl., the last verse of Psalm cl. is repeated. Lastly, the Memorial for the Departed, which figures at all Festivals,[1] is followed by the recital of Psalm cxlv.; the Memorial is, as a rule, read on the last day of a Festival.

The *special psalms* for the Festivals are as follows:—

On the first two days of *Passover*,[2] Psalms cv. ("O give thanks unto the Lord"), which tells of the deliverance from Egypt, and Psalm lxxx. ("Give ear, O shepherd of Israel"), respectively; this psalm also refers to the deliverance from Egypt in verse 8. On the last two days, Psalms lxxvii. ("I will cry unto God with my voice"), chosen on account of verse 11, and lxvi. ("Make a joyful noise unto God"), respectively, chosen on account of verses 5-12; these are all said at the Morning Service. At

[1] An exception to this is the New Year Festival, because the ten days of penitence, of which the first two are the two days of the New Year Festival, form *one* period, and terminate with the Day of Atonement, on which the Memorial Service is held.

[2] This Festival lasts eight days.

Pentecost[1] the proper Psalms for the two days respectively, which are sung at the Morning Service, are Psalm lxviii. ("Let God arise"), and Psalm xxix. ("Give unto the Lord"); the former of these is chosen because of the reference, in verse 8, to the presence of God on Mount Sinai, for, according to the ancient tradition, the Festival of Pentecost was kept as the birthday of the Law. For the same reason Psalm xxix. is a special psalm for this Festival, since the expression "The Voice of the Lord" occurs in it seven times; for the Law was given on Mount Sinai by the Voice of the Lord (*cp.* Exodus xix. 19, xx. 1).

On the two first days of the Feast of *Tabernacles*,[2] Psalms xlii., xliii., are said respectively; the former because of verse 4, where mention is made of "The voice of joy and praise, a multitude keeping holy day;" the second because of the reference, in verse 3, to "tabernacles." On the last day of this Feast, Psalm xii. is said; this day is also called *Simcath Torah* ("The Rejoicing of the Law"), which is observed because it is the day on which the cycle of the readings from the Law is completed for the year. Psalm xii. is, therefore, chosen for this day because of verses 6, 7, "The words of the Lord are pure words . . ."

[1] This Festival lasts two days; it is also called *Shabuoth* (the Feast of "Weeks").

[2] This Feast last eight days; it is also called *Sukkoth* ("Booths")

The special Psalm for the *New Year Festival* is lxxxi., because of verse 8, "Hear, O My people, and I will testify unto thee," which contains the thought of judgement (see above). As this Festival falls within the penitential season, there is also a special "psalm of penitence," viz., Psalm xxvii., see verses 7-14. On New Year's Day the *shôphar* ("ram's horn") is blown in order to arouse people to repentance (so the Mishna, *Taanith* i. 6); prior to its sounding, the following versicle is said :—"Blessed is the people that knoweth the trumpet sound, they walk, O Lord, in the light of Thy countenance;" then Psalm xlvii. is said, in which mention is made of the trumpet in verse 5: "God is gone up with a shout, the Lord with the sound of the trumpet."

At *New Moon Festivals* Psalm civ. is used because the New Moon is a symbol of God's Providence in renewing the face of the earth (see verses 19, 31). At the Festival of *Channukah* ("Dedication")[1] Psalm xxx. is chanted verse by verse alternately by the *Chazzan* and the congregation; this practice is very ancient. The title of this Psalm has, "A Song at the Dedication of the House," and according to *Sopherim* xviii. 2, the Levites sang it in the Temple.

At the Feast of *Purim*, Psalm vii. is said; and on *Shushan Purim*[2] Psalm lx.

[1] Also called the "Feast of the Maccabees," see 1 Macc. iv. 59.

[2] *I.e.*, the day following the Feast of *Purim*.

In the Sephardic Ritual the Festival psalms are as follows:—

At *Passover*, on the eve of the Festival, Psalms cvii., cxiii.-cxviii. (Hallel), are said, while cxiv. is repeated at the end of the service. During Morning Service Psalm cvii. is said, also the Hallel, complete, on the two first days, and half-Hallel on the middle and last two days; at the Afternoon Service Psalm cvii. is again said. On the Sabbath that falls within this Festival, Psalm xciii. is chanted after the reading of the Law; if the Sabbath falls on one of the middle days of the Festival, then Psalm cxi. is chanted. The psalms for the Evening Service are the same as those for the eve of the Festival. The special psalm for *Pentecost* is lxviii., which is used at all four services; besides this, Psalm cxxii. is said on the eve, and the complete Hallel at Morning Service. At *Tabernacles* Psalms xlii., xliii. are said at all services, Psalm cxxii. at the eve, and Psalm xii. at the Afternoon Service if a Sabbath; Hallel is said at Morning Service. On the eighth day of the Festival Psalm xii. is said in place of Psalms xlii., xliii.; on *Simcath Torah* the service is the same as on the eighth day. The special Psalms at the *New Year Festival* are cxlv., xxv., cxxx., and at the Afternoon Service Psalm lxxxi. At *New Moon Festivals* Psalm civ. is said on the Eve, excepting when this falls on a Friday; Hallel is said at Morning Service, omitting Psalms cxiv., cxv. At the *Channukah*

Festival Psalm xxx. is said at the Evening Service, and the complete Hallel at the Morning Service. Finally, at the *Feast of Purim*, Psalms cxxiv., xxii. are said on the Eve, Psalm xxii. at the Morning Service, and Psalm cxxiv. at Afternoon Service; while at the Morning Service on the day following after the Feast Psalm xxii. is again said.

Within recent times the Sephardic Jews have included in their Ritual Psalms xli., cxii. at the service for a Hospital Fund; the Ashkenazic Jews use the latter on this occasion. It will thus be seen that in some respects the two Rituals vary, while in others they agree; there can, however, be little doubt that in many cases both Rituals follow a common and very ancient tradition.

§ IV. *The Psalms on the Fast Days.*

The chief Fast in the Jewish Church is the *Day of Atonement*[1]; on the eve of this day, the special Psalm is cxix., which is *said*. On the day itself, in the Ashkenazic Ritual, in addition to the usual Psalms at the Morning Service, Psalm xxxii. is said, and Psalm xxvii. is the special "penitential psalm." But an alternate use, which obtains in this country, is the saying of Psalm lxv. as the special psalm for this day. Towards the end of the Evening Service, on the termination of this

[1] Some Jews cite Psalm xxxv. 13 as one reason of absolute fasting on this day.

Fast, Psalm cxxviii. is said. The Memorial of the Departed is said at this Fast, and it is followed by Psalms xvi. and cxlv. At the conclusion of this Fast the *shôphar* is blown as a final call to repentance.[1] In the Sephardic Ritual Psalms xxxiii., i.-iv., are said on the eve of the Fast, while at the Morning Service on the Fast-day itself the following Psalms are said:—xvii., xxv., xxxii., li., lxv., lxxxv., lxxxvi., cii., civ. xcviii. At the Morning Service of the day following the Fast, Psalm lxxxv. is again said.

The lesser Fasts in the Jewish Church are:

The Fast of *Gedaliah;* this is observed in memory of Gedaliah, the son of Ahikam, who was murdered by Ishmael (Jeremiah xli. 2). The Ashkenazic Jews have no special psalm for this fast, but Psalms x., xxvii. are the special ones for the ten days of penitence, *i.e.* from New Year to the Day of Atonement. The Sephardic Jews use Psalms xxv., xx., lxxxiii. at Morning Service, and xx., xxv., cii. at Afternoon Service; these are also the special psalms for all the minor fasts.

The Fast of *Tebeth* is kept in memory of the commencement of the siege of Jerusalem. According to the Ashkenazic Ritual, Psalm lxxiv. is the proper one; according to the Sephardic, Psalm lxxxiii. at Morning Service, and Psalm cxxvi. at Afternoon Service.

[1] The Synagogue also understands the *shôphar*-call as a joyful sign of God's pardon.

The Fast of *Esther;* the thirteenth of the month Adar, on which this fast is kept, is the traditional day which Ahasuerus, instigated by Haman, appointed for the slaughter of the Jews (see Esther iii. 13). Psalm xxii. is the appointed psalm among the Ashkenazim; Psalms cxxiv., cxxii. at Morning Service, Psalm xxiv. at Afternoon Service, among the Sephardim.

The Fast of *Tammuz.* This fast is observed in memory of the first breach made in the wall during the siege of Jerusalem; according to both Rituals the special Psalm is lxxix.

The Fast of *Ab.* According to the Rabbinical tradition, both temples were destroyed on the ninth of the month Ab, hence the observance of a fast on this day. The Ashkenazim use Psalm cxxxvii. as the special one, the Sephardim use this at Morning Service, and Psalm lxxix. at Evening Service.

It would, no doubt, have been of interest to have specified at what particular parts of the different services the various Psalms occur; but this would have involved a detailed description of the structure of the services themselves, which is not our present concern, and which would, moreover, have taken up a great deal of space.

V. *The method of rendering the Psalms in the modern Synagogue.*

It will have been noticed that we have referred

above to the Psalms sometimes as having been said, at other times as having been sung; as a matter of fact, there are no fixed rules for the rendering of the Psalms, but there are a number of customs regarding this, of which the following are the chief:—

At festivals the only psalms *sung* are parts of the Hallel, but the first and last verses of every psalm are sung by the Reader; this latter is also the case at ordinary times. The Sephardic Jews *read* the entire services. Then again, some psalms, *e.g.* the Hallel[1] and Psalms cxliv., lxvii., are sung either entirely by the congregation, or, as in the case of the Hallel, the Reader sings each verse, and the congregation repeats it after him. Psalm cxlv. is also, in some Congregations, sung verse by verse by the Reader and the congregation, or by the choir. The Psalms on Friday night are chanted alternately by the Reader and the congregation. It was an old custom, no more observed, however, for a special official to read Psalms before Morning Service every day in the synagogue.

In the synagogues ot orthodox Congregations there is no organ, the singing being entirely unaccompanied; but this has, apparently, not always been the universal rule, for Zunz mentions that one of the synagogues in Prague has possessed an organ for centuries. In 1716 a new organ was built for

[1] See what was said on p. 163 on the way the Hallel is sung.

this synagogue.[1] It may be added that, according to Müller,[2] the ordinary daily psalms were said, or sung, *sitting*, but on the festivals the congregation *stood* during psalms, whether sung or said. It will not be without interest to give an example of a melody used in the modern Synagogue, taken from De Sola's *The Ancient Melodies of the Spanish and Portuguese Jews;* it certainly has an antique ring about it :—

[1] *Op. cit.*, p. 491.

[2] In the notes to his edition of *Sopherim*, xviii. 2.

CHAPTER X.

THE PSALMS IN PRIVATE USE.

§ I. *The private use of psalms among the ancient Israelites.*

In dealing with the question of the gradual growth of the Psalter and the various elements contained in it, Dean Kirkpatrick says: "The various *strata* of which it is composed can to some extent be distinguished. Three principal divisions, marked by well-defined characteristics, may be observed . . . Speaking broadly and generally, the psalms of the first division are *personal*, those of the second, *national*, those of the third, *liturgical.* There are numerous exceptions, but it is in the first division that personal prayers and thanksgivings are chiefly to be found."[1] The *personal* psalms here referred to are such as iii., iv., v. (in part), vi., viii., xi., xiii., xvi., xviii., xxii., xxiii., and others, in which the first person singular is used. Many critics are against the view that such psalms refer to the individual; they hold that these are rather meant to express the feelings and

[1] *The Book of Psalms*, I. pp. xxxix. ff.

thoughts of the Israelite community personified. Cheyne, for example, maintains that "in the psalmists, as such, the individual consciousness was all but lost in the corporate; the Psalter is a monument of Church-consciousness."[1] There is, however, a good deal to be said in favour of the other view, that most of the "I" psalms were originally, and, in their essence, still are, devotions of a purely personal character;[2] this does not mean to say that they were not used, even when first composed, in the Temple-worship; but they were used there, not as part of a liturgical service, but for the edification of the individual worshipper, and as the expression of individual devotion. What seems to be quite certain is that a number of psalms which were originally composed for private use, were in later days, adapted to public worship; hence the liturgical titles which have been added to them. What is, however, here laid stress upon, is that from very early times—it is, of course, impossible to assign any particular period as that during which this first commenced—the private use of psalms has been in vogue among the Hebrews. The point is, perhaps, obvious; but it is well to insist upon it, for it is

[1] *Origin of the Psalter*, p. 265; *cp.* also Smend in the *Zeitschrift für die alttestamentliche Wissenschaft*, 1888, pp. 49 ff.

[2] It is, of course, not denied that such Psalms, *e.g.* as xliv., lvii., lix., lxvi., and others, are national, although the first person singular occurs in them.

illustrated, as we shall see, in a strange way in later times; it is still the custom among the Jews; and it explains, in part, the, comparatively speaking, small number of psalms in use in the public worship of the modern Synagogue.

Personal communion with God was a characteristic of the pious Israelite; in spite of the acknowledged fact that the importance of the individual was regarded as nothing in comparison with that of the community, the individual did not, so far as he *himself* was concerned, lay too much stress upon this. Where his personal relationship with his God was in question, there personal religion was supreme; and the fact of the existence of that relationship must have needed outward expression. When, for example, a worshipper brought an offering he would want to express his feelings towards God in words. This can be illustrated by what we are told in the Mishna (*Shebuoth* ii. 2), namely, that during the offering of "cakes of unleavened bread" (see Lev. vii. 13) the Levites sang Psalm xxx. to the accompaniment of instrumental music; by this means the feelings of each individual worshipper was outwardly expressed in words. This desire would be especially prominent in the case of petitions and of thank-offerings, see, for example, 1 Samuel i. 10, 11, ii. 1-10.[1] These would be examples of the beginnings of the use of private

[1] This "Song of Hannah" in its present form, at any rate, is late.

psalms, many of which would have become stereotyped when handed down from parent to child. It is, therefore, difficult to resist the conviction that in the Psalter we have adaptations of some very early psalms expressive of individual worship, which, being the outpouring of personal feeling, were intended for private use. For example, an individual note is clearly sounded in xxv. 4, 5: "Shew me Thy ways, O Lord; teach me Thy paths. Guide me in the truth, and teach me, for Thou art the God of my salvation; on Thee do I wait all the day;" *cp.* also v. 1-8, vi., vii. 17, xiii. 6, xviii. (see esp. ver. 6), xxi. 13, xxiii., xxvi., xxxii. 11, lv., etc., etc. We have, moreover, at least one striking example of a private psalm outside the Psalter, which may well illustrate the way in which psalms were written on special occasions by individuals, for their own comfort or edification in the first instance, and which were afterwards adapted for more general use. The psalm in 2 Samuel i. 19-27 ("David's Lament over Saul and Jonathan") was, on the face of it, originally written to express the writer's individual feelings. Psalms like this, which must have been transmitted orally for a long time before they were committed to writing, are scarcely likely to have come down to us in their original form. That in some form or other this poem was actually composed by David need not be doubted. In the case of this particular psalm there is internal evidence of its having been originally written for private use as a commemoration of the dead, and that only in later days it became incorporated, in written form, in the Book of Jashar. In verse 17 of this chapter this psalm is called a *Kinah*, the technical term for a "lamentation;" but, strange to say, it is not written in the ordinary *Kinah*-measure (see above p. 102), which we should naturally expect. The reason for this cannot be that the *Kinah*-measure was unknown in the time of David, for it was probably known long before this time, but because "we are concerned here not with the official, stereotyped measure of the wailing women, but with one which was exceptional, and individual;" for which reason this lamentation was purposely made to differ in form from the ordinary popular *Kinah*-measure, and was composed in a rhythmical form corresponding to the free and unfettered play of personal emotion.[1] If psalms such as these, therefore, were used privately—psalms which were of an almost wholly secular character—it is certain that there must have been many whose content was purely religious which were likewise written for private use; the fact that many of these came in course of time to be used in public worship only proves how widespread their use as private psalms must once have been.

[1] See Budde in the *Zeitschrift für die alttestamentliche Wissenschaft*, ii. pp. 44 ff.

In the Psalter we have, then, a number of psalms which were originally composed for private use some of these were adapted for liturgical use in the Temple worship; others were incorporated into the collection, but were never used in public worship, nor were they ever intended to be.

§ II. *The private use of psalms among the Jews.*

Among the Jews, from post-biblical times onwards, the Psalms have played a large part in private life; in many respects this private use of the Psalms, like their use in the modern Synagogue, reflects pre-Christian usage. Attention may, however, first be drawn to a fact, which is not without significance, namely, the, comparatively speaking, limited number of psalms which, as we have already seen, are in use in the modern Synagogue-worship. Of the seventy-three, moreover, which are used in the Ashkenazic Ritual, only fifteen belong to Book i, which confessedly contains the largest number of "I" psalms; and of these fifteen, only seven (vi., viii., xvi., xxv., xxvii., xxx., xxxviii.) can be reckoned among the "I" psalms. This seems to point to the fact that the majority of the psalms belonging to this type were not used in the Temple-worship, upon which the Synagogue-worship is based. On the other hand, practically all the psalms are for one purpose or another used in private. But before dealing with this private use of the psalms in some detail, it is worth while making mention of the custom, which grew up among the Jews, during the early Middle Ages, of incorporating certain hymns into the Synagogue-worship.[1] The object of drawing attention to this (which does not strictly belong to the subject of this chapter) is that it offers an interesting analogy of the way in which many of the psalms became adapted for public worship, though not originally intended for this. Perhaps these later Jewish poets were following on the lines of traditional custom, in which case their action assumes a still greater interest. This later form of psalm is known as a *Piyyut* (plural *Piyyutim*); "the word is derived from the Greek term for poetry, perhaps more directly

[1] The suggestion may, however, be hazarded that hymns of this kind were also composed at a much earlier period. The early Church was indebted to the Jewish in most respects as regards public worship, and there is evidence that in the public worship of the Church, hymns, which evidently corresponded to the later *Piyyutim* of the Jewish Church, were in use; thus, the fifty-ninth canon of the council of Laodicæa (363 A.D.) forbids the recitation of "private" psalms in the church, and "the Muratorian Fragment, a damaged document of the beginning of the third century, in distinguishing books which ought to be received into the Church for public use from others, repudiates with vigour a certain 'new book of the psalms'" (Prof. E. Barnes in the *Expositor* for July, 1910, pp. 53 ff.). The "Odes and Psalms of Solomon," recently discovered and published by Dr. J. Rendel Harris, a Christian Hymn-Book belonging to the third century A.D. (perhaps earlier), is a very interesting illustration of what has been said. It is, as suggested, quite possible that this custom in the early Church was founded upon something analogous in the Jewish Church; in this case, the *Piyyutim* of the Middle Ages would be the later representatives of antecedents of earlier date.

from *poiētēs* ('a poet'). The author of a *piyyut* is called a *payyetan*, a Neo-Hebrew form derived from *piyyut*."[1] The vast majority of *Piyyutim*[2] have not been incorporated into the Liturgy; herein also they offer an analogy to the Psalms; for it may be taken for granted that in the Psalter we have but a fraction of the psalms which must have accumulated during the many generations which preceded its final redaction. The *Piyyutim* were added to the older Liturgy that developed during the Talmudic era up to the seventh century A.D.; "the oldest are anonymous, they were written during the era of the early Geonim (*circa*, 7th cen.), and are embodied in the Prayer Book. They show an attempt at metre, and, as in some late Biblical poetical compositions, are often alphabetically arranged. . . It seems likely that they (*i.e.* the authors) were influenced by the troubadours and the minnesingers, both in the writing of their poems and in their musical settings."[3] *Piyyutim* were also written for private use in the homes.[4] As an example of part of a *Piyyut* we may give a few of the opening lines of "Hakol Joduka," which is recited during the Morning Service for Sabbaths and Festivals:

> "All shall thank Thee, and all shall praise Thee,
> And all shall say, 'None is holy as the Lord'!
> All shall exalt Thee, Maker of all,
> Thou God that openest daily the doors of the gates of the east;

[1] *Jewish Encycl.* x. 65 *b*. [2] The names of over 900 *Payyetanim* are known. [3] *Ibid.* Zunz, *Op. cit.* p. 406.

That cleavest the windows of the firmament,
That bringest forth the sun from his place, and the moon from her dwelling:
That givest light to the whole world and the inhabitants thereof,
Whom thou didst create by Thy attribute of mercy."

A number of fragments of ancient *Piyyutim* have been found in recent times in the Cairo Genizah.[1] Concerning these Schechter writes that one "can see by their abruptness and their unfinished state that they were not the product of elaborate literary art, but were penned down in the excitement of the moment, in a 'fit of love,' so to speak, to express the religious aspirations of the writer. Their metre may be faulty, their diction crude, and their grammar questionable; but love-letters are not, as a rule, distinguished by perfection of style. They are sublime stammering at best, though they are intelligible enough to two souls absorbed in each other. I am particularly fond of looking at the remnants of a Piyyutim collection, written on papyrus leaves, with their rough edges and very ancient writing. In turning over those leaves, with which time has dealt so harshly, one almost imagines one sees again 'the gods ascending out of the earth,' transporting us, as they do, to the Kaliric[2] period, and perhaps even earlier. . ."[3]

[1] A kind of lumber room which adjoins the synagogue.

[2] Kalir was the most popular of all the *Piyyutim* writers; he lived during the ninth century. [3] *Studies in Judaism* (Second Series), pp. 18 f.

It should be added that the later *Piyyutim* have never been looked upon with great favour by the Jewish ecclesiastical authorities; their use has, at certain periods, been acquiesced in as a concession to popular fancy. "The degree of approval with which these hymns were received, or of personal respect which the author, in many instances a local Rabbi, enjoyed, decided for or against the insertion of the *Piyyutim* in the Machzor [*i.e.*, Ritual] of the congregation. Opposition to the inclusion of the *Piyyut* in the regular prayer as an unlawful interruption of divine service is found as early as the eleventh century."[1] A collection of hostile criticisms on the poetic effusions of the *Payyetanim* is contained in A. A. Wolf's *Stimmen der ältesten Rabbinen über die Payyetanim* (1867).[2]

But we must turn again now from these more or less unsuccessful imitations to the Psalms themselves, in order to give a few details as to their private use among the Jews since post-biblical times. We shall give examples of psalms, or verses from the psalms, in quasi-private use, as well as their purely private use by individuals. An instance of the former, which was so far private in that it was used for the benefit of an individual, though said in the synagogue, we may give Psalm lxxviii. 38, "But He, being full of

[1] *Jewish Encycl.* x. 67 *b*.

[2] My attention was drawn to this work by the Rev. G. E. Friedlander.

compassion, forgave their iniquity, and destroyed them not; yea, many a time turned He His anger away, and did not stir up all His wrath." This was preceded by Deut. xxviii. 58, 59, xxix. 8, and these four verses were said over and over again during a scourging. The scourging consisted of forty strokes save one[1] (*cp.* 2 Cor. xi. 24); it took place in the synagogue (*cp.* Matthew x. 17, Acts xxii. 19), and the punishment was inflicted by a synagogue official called the *Chazzan.*[2]

Certain psalms have, from time immemorial, been used during the Occasional Offices in the Synagogue; these are, of course, in a sense, used publicly, but they may be mentioned here inasmuch as these services concern individuals rather than the congregation. Thus, at a Circumcision the Sephardic Jews use Psalm cxxviii. ("Blessed is everyone that feareth the Lord"); the Ashkenazic Jews use Psalm xii. ("Help, Lord, for the godly man ceaseth"; see esp. vv. 5-7); but with them the *Mohel,*[3] on receiving the child from the hands of the father, recites the following verses, in this order: Psalm cxix. 166, 162, 165, and the first two clauses of lxv. 4, whereupon those present respond with the two last clauses of this verse. Further, the Marriage Service opens

[1] The number of strokes was not, according to the Law, to exceed forty (Deut. xxxv. 2, 3), thirty-nine were, therefore, given in order to ensure that the forty would not be exceeded (*Makkoth* iii. 10).

[2] Mishna, *Makkoth* iii. 14.

I.e., the accredited official licensed to perform the act of circumcision.

with the versicles: "Blessed be he that cometh in the name of the Lord; we have blessed you out of the house of the Lord" (Psalm cxviii. 26); "O come, let us worship and bow down; let us kneel before the Lord our Maker" (Psalm xcv. 6); "Serve the Lord with joy; come before Him with exalting" (*cp.* Psalms ii. 11, xcv. 2). These are followed by Psalm c., "Shout for joy unto the Lord, all the earth." At the conclusion of the service, after the Blessing has been given, Psalm cl., "Praise ye the Lord," is said. Again, it is a touching custom according to which a husband recites frequently Psalm cxxviii. when the time is drawing near for his wife to be delivered of a child; the appropriateness of this will be seen on reading the psalm. At the Burial Service Psalm xvi. is said ("Preserve me, O Lord, for in Thee do I put my trust"); this is the case among the Sephardic as well as the Ashkenazic Jews. In the Sephardic Ritual, when the coffin is being lowered into the grave, Psalm xci. is said ("He that dwelleth in the secret place of the Most High"). The Ashkenazic Jews, on leaving the burial-ground, say either: "And they of the city shall flourish like the grass of the earth" (Psalm ciii. 15), or, "He remembereth that we are dust" (Psalm ciii. 14). More specifically of a private character is the use of Psalms i., xv., xvi., xc., xci., which are said when a tombstone is set up; the Sephardic Jews use only the last three of these. In the house of mourning either Psalm xvi., or Psalm xlix. (on account of verses 7-10, 12, 15) is said; the latter, together with some of the sections of Psalm cxix.,[1] is also said by the Sephardic Jews. In addition to the above, the Ashkenazic Jews sometimes also repeat Psalms xv., xxxix., xc., xci., ciii., in the house of mourning.

It is the echo of an extremely ancient custom that a private service is held at the consecration of a house; at this service Psalms xv., xxx., ci., cxxi., are said, as well as Psalms cxxvii., cxxviii., if they are appropriate (see cxxvii. 3-5, cxxviii. 3-6, where there is the mention of children); besides these, four sections of Psalm cxix. are said, viz., verses 9-16, 153-160, 81-88, 33-40; they are said in this order, as the initial letters of each verse of these different sections form the Hebrew word, "Blessing." The Sephardic Jews on this occasion use only Psalm xxx. ("I will extol thee, O Lord, for Thou hast raised me up"), and Psalm cxxxiv. ("Behold, bless ye the Lord, all ye servants of the Lord").

Again, those who are sick are urged to use Psalms xxiii. ("The Lord is my Shepherd"), ciii. ("Bless the Lord, O my soul"), and cxxxix. ("O Lord, Thou hast searched me out and known me").

A special Psalm, cxxvi., is appointed to be said at grace before or after meals, the custom varies; some-

[1] Those sections are chosen the initial letters of which make up the name of the departed; on the acrostic character of this psalm, see p. 108.

times this is sung. Before retiring to rest Psalms xci. and iii. are said both by Ashkenazic and Sephardic Jews. Psalm xci., followed by Psalm cxxi. (both of which are extremely appropriate to the occasion), are said by one undertaking a journey. Among the Sephardic Jews, if a man desires to exercise a voluntary fast, *i.e.*, one in addition to those appointed, he recites Psalm cii. (see especially verse 4).

It will have been noticed what a prominent place Psalm cxlv. has in the Services of the Synagogue; it is worth while noting, in connexion with this, that it is the conviction of many Jews that anyone who recites this psalm devoutly three times a day is sure of going to heaven.[1] Another example of the private use of a psalm is that of Psalm xxx.; many Jews repeat this while "laying the Tephillin;" this is the technical term used for binding on the head- and the hand-Tephillah (= "Phylactery"). Again, young children are taught, in the course of their night-prayer, to say: "Behold, he that guardeth Israel will neither slumber nor sleep" (Psalm cxxi. 4), "Into Thy hand I commend my spirit; Thou hast redeemed me, O Lord God of truth" (Psalm xxxi. 5); and they conclude with the words: "For Thy salvation I hope, O Lord" (Psalm cxix. 166).

There is, once more, a custom, by no means universal, but nevertheless in wide use, of reading the Psalms in the home (sometimes also privately

[1] See p. 156.

in the synagogue), so as to complete the Psalter within a set period; this period may be a month, or a week, or even one day, *i.e.*, the Sabbath.[1]

A curious custom is that of saying Psalms cxlviii., cl., lxvii. at the Blessing of the New Moon; it is always said on a Sabbath night before the 14th of the month, and the Blessing must be said out of doors. In the Babylonian Talmud (*Sanhedrin*, 42 *a*) it is said in reference to this: "He who says this Benediction is accounted as though he had received the presence of the *Shekhina*."[2]

It should also be mentioned here that some other Psalms are used in a quasi-private way since they are recited during that part of the Passover celebration which takes place in the home. This home-service is called the *Haggadah* ("Announcement," viz., of God's mercies to Israel). During this service, after the drinking of the first cup of wine, the first two psalms of the "Hallel" (Psalms cxiii., cxiv.) are said; this applies to both Ashkenazim and Sephardim. Before the "Blessing after meat," which precedes the drinking of the third cup, another psalm is said; the Ashkenazic Jews say Psalm cxxi., the Sephardic Psalm cvii. The fourth cup is then filled, and the remaining psalms of the "Hallel" are said, viz.: cxv., cxvi., this latter, in verse 13, speaks of the "taking up of the cup of salvation," cxvii., the invitation to the Gentiles, and cxviii. Then, after

[1] *Cp.* p. 155 above.

[2] *I.e.*, The Divine Glory,

a hymn ("All Thy works praise Thee"), the "Great Hallel," Psalm cxxxvi., is said. All these last five psalms are said by both the Ashkenazic and Sephardic Jews.

§ III. *Sepher Shimmush Tehillim.*

Certainly, the quaintest use, private or otherwise, to which the Psalms have ever been put is that which is recommended in the above-mentioned book, a recommendation which has been acted upon for generations by numbers of Jews living in the Eastern parts of Europe, mainly, though in the Western parts as well. The superstition of very many of these Jews is well known, but the fact that the "Shimmush Tehillim" exists also in an English translation points to a demand which is not confined to the Jews of Poland or Roumania. Prof. Ludwig Blau, who has made a great study of these things, writes as follows: "Next to the Torah, the Psalms were especially popular in magic, since they formed the real book of the people, one which they knew and loved as a book of prayers; and prayers had, according to the popular opinion of the ancients, extremely close affinities with incantations . . . Tablets inscribed with verses of the Psalms or of the Bible generally, and found in great numbers in recent years, must have been regarded as a means of protection for both the living and the dead . . . No other ancient examples of this use of the Psalms are known; but in the Middle Ages the employment of the Psalms in all the vicissitudes of life was so extensive and detailed that there is no doubt that it was based on ancient custom . . . In all probability the origin of the employment of the Psalms in magic is essentially Jewish."[1] Evidently, therefore, the directions given in the "Shimmush Tehillim" may, in one form or another, be traced back to a high antiquity; indeed, in more than one case, this can be proved (see under Psalm xxix., p. 194). The name *Sepher Shimmush Tehillim* means, "The Book of the use of the Psalms"; on the title-page of the English translation it is stated to be: "A fragment out of the Practical Kabbala; together with an extract from a few other Kabbalistic writings of the old wise Hebrews, taken from the Mosaic books of the Kabbala and the Talmud for the good of mankind." The translator concludes his Preface with the following words: "I confidently hope and trust, and I can assert without hesitation, that this little book cannot have a tendency to foster superstition. Take it for granted that one of my readers should choose to employ one of the methods described in these pages in order to accomplish a desired object, his eagerness to satisfy curiosity will soon disappear when he takes into

[1] *Jewish Encycl.* x. pp. 240, 241.

[2] See also the Commentary on Psalm xci., Chap. xii.

consideration the hard terms and strict morality which are required to avail himself of them in order to derive any benefit or be successful in their use." As will be seen from some of the extracts from this work to be given presently, it is difficult to understand how anyone at the present day can take the suggested methods seriously; yet this translator does so, and he represents a multitude of men and women who think likewise. But, after all, it is well to remember that superstitious beliefs, and crass practices based on them, are by no means confined to any one age or to any one race. There is probably not a country district in any land in Europe, let alone uncivilized countries, in which such things are not rife at the present day. The details to be given represent, therefore, illustrations of what is only a somewhat extreme form of widely prevalent beliefs and practices; the particular point of interest about the ones with which we are here concerned is that they all deal with the Psalms. The Preface to the *Sefer Shimmush Tehillim* gives some insight into the reason why this book has been in such vogue among certain classes of Jews, for the directions it contains are believed to have come, at least indirectly, from the Almighty Himself. "It is universally known and acknowledged that we are named after the most holy name of the Ruler of the World, and that we receive the holy decalogue, or the written Law, from Him. It is further well known that in addition to the laws which He gave to Moses engraven upon stone, He also gave to him certain verbal laws, by which, through his protracted stay upon the mountain Sinai, where all doctrines, explanations of mysteries, holy names of God and the angels, and particularly how to apply this knowledge to the best interests of man, were entrusted to him. . . Therefore do we know that in the Torah are many names of the Most High and His angels, besides deep mysteries, which may be applied to the welfare of man, but which on account of the perverseness of humanity, and to guard against their abuse, have been hidden from the great mass of human beings." After going on to show that "the Psalms and the Torah are equal in holiness and worthiness," it continues: "Through a pious life and by a rational use of the Psalms you may obtain the grace of God, the favour of princes and magistrates, and the love of your fellow-men. You will be enabled to protect yourself from danger, to escape suffering, and to promote your own welfare. That this is all true, the contents of each prayer with which we end each psalm, and which we are in duty bound to pray, will amply demonstrate. But the correctness of it is also established by the teachings of the Talmud and of the old wise men, who assure us that many of our famous forefathers availed themselves of apparently supernatural means from time to time to protect their best interests. The truth of this I can establish by the most trustworthy witnesses;

yea, I could even mention some great men, who, by a proper use of the Psalms, performed great works."

It is our intention to give only a few examples from this extraordinary book; but it must be remembered that every one of the 150 psalms is mentioned in order, together with the malady or misfortune for which its "correct" recital is a specific.

Under *Psalm iii.* it is said: "Whosoever is subject to severe headache and backache, let him pray this psalm, with the leading holy names and appropriate prayer contained therein, over a small quantity of olive oil; anoint the head and back while in the act of prayer.[1] This will afford immediate relief. The holy name is *Adon* ('Lord'), and is found in the words: We*a*tt*a* ('But Thou,' ver. 3, in Hebrew ver. 4), Baa*d*i ('About me,' ver. 3), Hekiz*o*ti ('I awaked,' ver. 5, in Hebrew ver. 6), Hashie*n*i ('Save me,' ver. 7, in Hebrew ver. 8)."[2] Then follows the prayer. *Psalm vi.* is believed to be efficacious for all the diseases of the eye, a simpler prescription than that given by the angel Azarias to Tobias (see Tobit vi. 8, xi. 11-13). The direction here given is: "Read the psalm for three days successively, and pray the prescribed prayer seven times slowly, in a low tone, and with devotion;

[1] *Cp.* James v. 14.

[2] We have italicized the letters which go to make up the "Holy Name," *Adon.*

and with this keep continually in your mind the holy name of *Jeshajah*, which means 'help is with the Lord';[1] believe without a doubt that the Lord can and will help you." Concerning *Psalm vii.* it is said: "When evil persons conspire to render you unfortunate . . . then take, upon the spot where you stand, a handful of earth or dust, pray this psalm, and keep in your mind the holy name *El Elyon*, 'Great, strong, highest God;' then throw the dust in the direction of your enemies, uttering a prayer prescribed for this case, and you will see that your enemies will cease their persecutions, and leave you undisturbed." The prescribed prayer then follows. *Psalm ix.* can be used as a cure for sick boys; it has to be written on pure parchment, with a new pen, and hung round the neck of the sufferer. Concerning *Psalm x.* it is said: "If anyone is plagued with an unclean, restless, and evil spirit, let him fill a new earthen pot with water from the spring, and, in the name of the patient, pour it into pure olive oil, and pronounce over it this psalm nine times . . ." The belief that demons have a horror of water is extremely ancient and widespread.[2] *Psalm xvi.* is believed to have extraordinary power: "This psalm is important, and can be profitably employed on different undertakings. As for example, if anyone has been robbed, and wishes to

[1] The word means "The Lord hath saved;" it does not occur in the psalm, and is evidently an error; in the psalm the word is *Hoshieni*, "Save me."

[2] *Cp.* Matthew xii. 43; Luke xi. 24; see p. 195

know the name of the robber, he must proceed as follows :—Take mud or slime and sand out of a stream, mix them together; then write the names of all suspected persons upon small slips of paper, and apply the mixture on the reverse side of the slips; afterwards lay them in a large and clean basin, filled for this purpose with fresh water from the stream; lay them in the water one by one, and at the same time pray this psalm over them ten times, with the prayer adapted to it . . . if the name of the real thief is written upon the slips, that upon which the name is written will rise to the surface." Still more wonderful is the potency of *Psalm xix.*, this ensures a safe delivery after a dangerous confinement if the first five verses are written on earth taken from a cross-road, and the earth be then laid upon the woman. Moreover, a father can make his son an apt student by reciting this psalm over a cup filled with wine and honey; he must also pronounce the Holy Name, and say an appropriate prayer over the cup, the contents of which he must then give his son to drink. This psalm, when recited, is also efficacious in driving away evil spirits; the same is the case with *Psalm xxix.*, which is "highly recommended for casting out an evil spirit;" but the prescribed ritual here is somewhat complicated, it is as follows: "Take seven splinters of the osier, and seven leaves from a date-palm that never bore fruit, place them in a pot filled with water upon which the sun never shone, and repeat over it, in the evening, this psalm, with the most holy name of Aha, ten times with great reverence; and then, in full trust in the power of God, set the pot upon the earth in the open air, and let it remain there until the following evening. Afterwards pour the whole of it at the door of the possessed, and the evil spirit will surely depart." In the Midrash *Pesikta*, 112*a*, this psalm is recommended in order to avert the peril of drinking uncovered water in the dark on Wednesday evening, or on Sabbath eve;[1] drinking water at night is regarded as dangerous, presumably because the wrath of the evil spirit would be aroused by the use of water—the cleansing element—during his privileged period of activity, the night-time. Concerning *Psalm lviii.*, it is said: "If you should be attacked by a vicious dog, pray this psalm quickly, and the dog will not harm you"; the psalm is evidently chosen for this purpose because of the words in verse 6, "Break their teeth, O God, in their mouth." *Psalm cix.* may be efficaciously used in the following quaint connexion: "Have you a mighty enemy, who plagues and oppresses you, fill a new jug with new sparkling wine, add some mustard to it, then repeat this psalm three days successively, while, at the same time, you keep in mind the holy name of *El;* afterwards, pour the moisture before the door of your enemy's dwelling. Be careful, how-

[1] See *Jewish Encycl.*, x. 241*a*.

ever, that you do not sprinkle a single drop upon yourself when in the act of pouring it out."

Many more examples could, of course, be given; but enough has been quoted to show the extraordinary use to which the Psalms have been, and still are, sometimes put.

We do not profess to have given in this chapter an exhaustive account of the private use of the Psalms among the Jews, but it is hoped that some insight, at any rate, may have been gained regarding this part of our subject.

CHAPTER XI.

JEWISH EXEGESIS OF THE PSALMS.

THERE is no getting away from the fact that, in the main, Jewish exegesis of the Psalms is often artificial, sometimes trivial. We are, however, far from saying that *no* instruction is to be gained from the traditional interpretation of them in ancient Jewish literature. Some of the examples which we shall give will certainly be found to be not without an interest of their own; though, so far as the eludication of particular verses in the Psalms is concerned, it is but rarely that any real help is obtainable from ancient Jewish writers.[1] Nevertheless, a chapter devoted to Jewish exegesis seems not out of place, whatever the results may be, when seeking to gain some idea of the use of the Psalms in the Jewish Church.

The main source which has been utilised is the Midrash, or Homiletic Commentary, on the Psalms, known as *Midrash Tehillim*,[2] though a good deal of incidental use has been made of other Midrashic works,

[1] Modern Jewish scholars, with the exception o. Dr. Schiller-Szinessy who has edited part of Kimchi's work on the Psalms, have not, we venture to think, devoted sufficient attention to the study of the Psalms.

[2] In the following pages this will be referred to in the abbreviated form *Midr. T*

as well as appropriate passages from the Talmud, which have been picked up here, there and everywhere. The *Midr. T.* is very incomplete, for although every psalm receives more or less attention, it frequently happens that only a few verses of a psalm are commented on; this is very disappointing, and often mars the usefulness of the work. This *Midrash* originally dealt only with Psalms i-cxviii., and was written, according to Zunz[1], towards the end of the ninth century, A.D., though much material from older collections is incorporated in it[2]; the author is not known. Comments on the other Psalms were added later. It is partly homiletic, partly exegetic in character; it contains a large amount of interesting matter in the shape of parables, legends, proverbs, etc.[3] The following quotation (occurring in a comment on xxiv. i.) gives one a good idea of the artificial way in which Rabbinical exegesis is sometimes conducted; it purports to be a general rule: "Our Rabbis taught, 'Every verse which David uttered in the book of the Psalms, he spoke either in reference to himself, or in reference to all Israel. Every passage in which it is a question of one individual is in reference to himself; and every passage in which a number of men are spoken of is in reference to all Israel.'"

1 *Die gottesdienstlichen Vorträge der Juden*, p. 375.

2 *Jewish Encycl.* x. 248*b*.

3 The Hebrew text has been published by Buber, *Midr. T.* (1891); a German translation has been published by Wünsche (1892-1893).

Jewish Exegesis of the Psalms.

We shall divide the present chapter into the following sections: first, some examples of a miscellaneous character, in order to give some insight into the general method of Jewish exegesis; next, some examples to show the tendency to interpret passages in reference to the Torah, or Law; the third section will give some examples of Messianic interpretation; and in the last section some of the passages from the Psalms quoted in the New Testament will be briefly referred to.

§ I. *Some miscellaneous examples of Jewish exegesis.*

Psalm i. 1. As an example of the artificial way in which special words are sometimes treated reference may be made to the opening word of the Psalter, *Ashre* ("Blessed"), which, according to Rabbi Joshua ben Korcha, occurs twenty times in the book of Psalms, and corresponds with the twenty "Woes" in the book of Isaiah (*Midr. T.* i. 1).

Psalm ii. 12: "Kiss the son lest he be angry, and ye perish from the way."

In *Midr. T.* this verse is explained by a parable which is of great interest on account of the teaching on mediation it contains. It is said: "Whereunto is this to be compared? It is like a King who was wrath against the inhabitants of a city; these, therefore, went unto the King's son and made their peace with him, in order that he might go to the King and make peace on their behalf. So he went and pacified the King. When the inhabitants of that city knew that the King had been propitiated, they desired to sing a song (of thanksgiving) to him ; but he answered and said: 'Do ye wish to sing a song (of thanksgiving) to me? Nay, but go and sing it unto my son; for had it not been for him, I should have destroyed the inhabitants of the city.'"

Psalm vii. 15, 16: "He hath made a pit. . . ."

These verses are, appropriately enough, interpreted as referring to the overthrow of the Egyptians in the Red Sea, as described in Exod. xiv. 26ff (*Mechilta*[1] § vi.).

Psalm viii. 4-6: "What is man that thou art mindful of him. . . ."

In *Midr. T.* these verses are explained as follows: "What is man . . .": this refers to Abraham, as it is written in Gen. ix. 29; "And the son of man . . .": this refers to Isaac, as it is written in Gen. xxi. 1; "For thou hast made him . . .": this refers to Jacob, as it is written in Gen. xxx. 39[2]; "And crownest him . . .": this refers to Moses, as it is written in Exod. xxxiv. 29; "Thou madest him to have dominion . . .": this refers to Joshua, as it is written in Josh. x. 12, 13; "Thou hast put all things . . .": this refers

[1] A *Midrash* on Exodus.

[2] "Jacob was able to cause the flocks to bring forth ringstraked, speckled, and spotted, therein possessing almost divine power, but he was a little lower than God because he could not give them souls."

to David, as it is written in 2 Sam. xxii. 43; "All sheep and oxen": this refers to Solomon, as it is written in 1 Kings v. 13; "Yea, and the beasts of the field": this refers to Samson (see Judg. xv. 4, 5); "The fowl of the air": this refers to Elijah, as it is written in 1 Kings xvii. 6; "And the fish of the sea": this refers to Jonah, as it is written in Jonah ii. 1; "Whatsoever passeth . . .": this refers to the Israelites, as it is written in Exod. xv. 19.[1]

Psalm x. 3. "And the covetous renounceth, yea contemneth the Lord."

In *Sanhedrin* 6 *b* (Babylonian Talmud) this is rendered: "And he that blesseth the covetous contemneth the Lord"; but in *Midr. T.* it is rendered: "And the robber who blesses, blasphemes the Eternal," which is said to mean (according to Rabbi Eliezer ben Jacob) that if a man steals bread and offers a portion of it in sacrifice he becomes a blasphemer.

Psalm xi. 2: "For lo, the wicked bend the bow they make ready their arrow upon the string."

A good example of the freedom of Rabbinical exegesis is offered in the comment on this verse in *Sanhedrin* 26 *b*, where it is said: "During the siege of Jerusalem by Sennacherib, Shebna wrote a message and shot it with (*i.e.* attached to) an arrow; the message

[1] This passage has been considerably shortened; in the original the quotations are given in full.

ran, 'Shebna and his following (desire) to make peace with thee (*i.e.* with Sennacherib) and will capitulate, but Hezekiah and his following will not give in to thee,' according to Psalm xi. 2, 'For lo, the wicked . . .'"

Psalm xvi. 7: "My reins (*lit.* 'kidneys') instruct me in the night seasons."

This is quaintly interpreted by Rabbi Simeon ben Jochai, who taught that this verse shows that God gave Abraham two kidneys in the form of two pails, which poured wisdom and knowledge into him all night" (*Midr. T.* i. 1).

Psalm xxvii. 14: "Wait on the Lord; be strong, and let thine heart take courage."

Rabbi Chia the Great explained this verse in the words: "Pray, and again pray; the time will certainly come when thou wilt be heard"[1] (Midrash *Debarim Rabba* to iii. 24).

Psalm lxviii. 4 (in Heb. 5) "Cast up a highway for him that rideth in the deserts."

The interpretation of this passage is interesting from the point of view of the Jewish doctrine of God. According to Rabbinical teaching, there are above the earth seven heavens (*cp.* 2 Cor. xii. 2); God dwells in the highest, the seventh, which is called *Araboth.*[2]

[1] *Cp.* Luke xviii. 1 ff., 1 Thess. v. 17.

[2] Babylonian Talmud, *Chagigah* 12 *b.*

Now in the passage before us the Hebrew word for "the deserts" is *Araboth,* and the clause is rendered: "Extol Him that rideth upon Araboth," the following comment being added: "*Araboth* is the heaven in which are righteousness and grace, the treasures of life, the treasures of peace, and the treasures of bliss, and the souls of the righteous, and the souls and the spirits which are about to be created, and the dew with which the Holy One, blessed be He, is to revive the dead . . . and there are the Ophanim,[1] the Seraphim, and the holy Chayoth,[2] and the ministering angels, and the throne of glory, and the King, the living God, high and exalted, rests above them, as it is written,"[3] —then follows the verse under consideration, as though to substantiate what has been said.

Psalm lxviii. 6 (in Heb. 7): "God maketh the solitary to dwell in a house" (according to the original).

It is well-known that the saying: "Marriages are made in heaven" is of Rabbinic origin; the following interpretation and comment on this verse well illustrates this; it occurs in the Midrash *Bereshith Rabba,* § lxviii. (near the beginning): A matron asked Rabbi Joshua bar Chalaphtha in how many days God created the world; he answered: "In six days" (see

[1] The second order of angels in Jewish Angelology.

[2] The highest order of angels.

[3] Babylonian Talmud, *Chagigah* 12 *b*, 13 *a*, quoted by Schechter, *Some Aspects of Rabbinic Theology*, p. 28.

Ex. xxxi. 17). Thereupon she asked: "And what has He been doing since then?" The Rabbi replied: "He sits and arranges marriages (*lit.* He binds pairs); He decrees that the daughter of such an one shall become the wife of such an one, and the property of such and such an one shall come to such and such an one." Then the matron said: "Does He do nothing more than that? I can do that too? How many menservants and maidservants have I, all of whom I could with ease make husband and wife in an hour." "Easy as it may be for thee," rejoined the Rabbi, "for God it is as difficult as the cleaving of the Red Sea in twain." With these words, the Rabbi retired. But what did the matron do? She went and took a thousand menservants and a thousand maidservants, and made them stand up in two rows, and said: "This man shall take that maid, and this maid shall take that man," and thus she paired them all off in one evening. The next day they came to her; one man had a wound in his forehead, a maid appeared with only one eye, a third with a broken foot, and so on. The matron asked, "What is it you want?" One said: "I do not want him"; another said: "I do not want her." The matron sent at once for Rabbi Joshua bar Chalaphtha, and said to him: "Of a truth, there is no God like thy God; thy law is true and excellent; thou didst well." Then said Rabbi Joshua: "Did I not say to thee, easy as it may be for thee, for God it is as difficult as the cleaving of the Red Sea in twain?" But what is that God does here? He joins together man and wife even against their will; that is what is meant by the words in Psalm lxviii. 7: "He maketh the solitary to dwell in a house."

Psalm lxviii. 26: "Bless ye God in the congregations, even the Lord, ye that are of the fountain of Israel." Rabbi Meir interprets the word "fountain" as referring to the womb, saying: "They that were in the womb opened their mouth, and uttered the Song before God"; the reference is to the Song of Moses (Ex. xv. 1): "Then sang Moses and the children of Israel this song unto the Lord" (*Mechilta*, to xvi. 1).

Psalm lxxxii. 1: "God standeth in the congregation of God."

It is said in *Sanhedrin* 6 *b* (Babylonian Talmud) that judges must know who they are judging, in whose presence they are administering justice, and who it is that will one day punish them if they pronounce a false judgement. This is based on the above text, which is rendered: "The Judge standeth . . . ." This interpretation is interesting on account of "God" (*El*) being rendered "Judge"; for, from the context in the passage in the Talmud it is clear that by "Judge" here it is not God, but a judge in the ordinary sense that is intended. A parallel to this is Ex. xxi. 6, where *Elohim* ("God") is used in reference to earthly judges (*cp.* Ex. xxii. 8, and v. 6 of this psalm).

Psalm cxlvii. 4: "He telleth the number of the stars."

In *Sanhedrin* 39 *a* (Babylonian Talmud) the following story is told: An unbeliever once said to Rabbi Gamaliel, "It is written in Psalm cxlvii. 4: 'He telleth the number of the stars'; what is there wonderful in that? I, too, can count the stars." The Rabbi, in reply, put a number of quinces in a vessel which he caused to be rotated, and said: "Count these." The unbeliever said: "Hold the vessel still, then I shall be able to count them." Thereupon the Rabbi rejoined: "But the heavens, too, are constantly rotating." In spite of his limited astronomical knowledge the Rabbi's argument was sound, for he meant that if the man could not count the number of the quinces under his very eyes because they were being moved, he was quite mistaken in supposing he could count the distant stars. A greater knowledge of the actual facts would only have tended to strengthen his argument still further. According to another tradition the Rabbi's answer to the unbeliever was this: "Tell me how many double teeth you have in your mouth, and how many single ones." The man put his hand into his mouth and began counting; but the Rabbi broke in: "You do not even know what is in your own mouth, and yet you pretend to know what is in the heavens."

§ II. *Some examples of interpreting passages as referring to the Law.*

As one would expect, a large number of passages in the Psalms are interpreted as referring to the Law, or

Tôrah; in other cases words in the Psalms are paralleled by corresponding words in the Law; some of these examples of exegesis are distinctly interesting, while others are more quaint than edifying. A few instances may be given.

Psalm i. 2: "But his delight is in the law of the Lord, and in His law doth he meditate day and night." "This is what the Scripture (Isa. lv. 1.) refers to, 'Ho, everyone that thirsteth, come ye to the waters.' Just as the waters are given from heaven, as it is said (Jer. x. 13), 'When he uttereth his voice there is a tumult of waters in the heavens,' so were the words of the Tôrah given from heaven, as it is said (Ex. xx. 19), Ye have seen that I spoke with you from Heaven'"[1] (*Midr. T.* to 1, 2).

Psalm xxix. 11: "The Lord will give strength unto His people."

By "strength" is meant the Tôrah, or Law; so too in Psalm xcix. 4. "The King's strength also loveth judgement" (*Mechilta* to xv. 13).

The words in Psalm xl. 8, "Then said I, Lo, I am come, in the roll of the book it is written of me" (better: "It is prescribed to me"), are explained by a reference to Deut. xvii. 18: "And it shall be, when he (*i.e.* the

[1] This latter is not a quotation rom *Exodus*, but an inference from what is said in the verse referred to.

King) sitteth upon the throne of His kingdom, that he shall write him a copy of this Law in a book."

Psalm cxix. 126. "They have made void Thy Law." This is explained to mean that one might do violence to the *Law* at a time when it was necessary to work for God (so Rabbi Nathan in *Berachoth* ix. 5, Mishna); *i.e.*, according to Hoffman,[1] it is permissible to transgress a precept of the Tôrah in order to do something for God, *e.g.*, as Elijah did on Mount Carmel when he offered sacrifice (which for him was forbidden by the Law, as he was not a priest) in order to glorify the name of God.

In reference to Psalm cxxxvi. 6: "To him that spread forth the earth above the waters," it is said that just as the waters flow from one end of the earth to the other, so does the divine teaching, as contained in the Tôrah, flow from one end of the earth to another (Midrash *Shir Hashirim* to i. 2). So, too, in the same place in this Midrash, it is said that just as, according to Psalm xii. 6, the words of the Lord purify, so also do the words of the Tôrah purify; reference is also made to Psalm cxix. 140. A further comparison is given in reference to Psalm civ. 15; just as "wine maketh glad the heart of man," so does the Tôrah cheer men's hearts; and again, in reference to the same verse, the Tôrah, like oil, makes a man's face to shine (*ibid*). Once more, it is written in Psalm cxix. 105, "Thy word is a lamp unto my feet, and a light unto my path," this

[1] In his edition of *Berachoth*.

is likewise interpreted as referring to the Tôrah.[1] It may be added that the Tôrah is also compared to bread, so Prov. ix. 5 is interpreted (Midrash *Bereshith Rabba* to xxviii. 20). Comparisons like these have a special interest in view of the fact that in the Gospels we find similar comparisons used in reference to our Lord (see for comparison with "water," John iv. 4, vii. 38; with the "word of God," John i. 1 ff.; with "wine," John xv. 1, *cp.* John vi. 55, 56, Mark xii. 23-25; with "light," John i. 9, viii. 12; with "bread," John vi. 35, 48, 51, 58).

Psalm cxlviii. 13. "Let them praise the name of the Lord, for His name alone is exalted; His glory is above the earth and heaven."

The "exalting of the name of the Lord" was interpreted to mean the observance of the Law, and "his glory" the *Shekhinah;* this verse is therefore explained by saying that, "Wherever the Law of God rested there also did His *Shekhinah* rest" (Midrash, *Shir Hashirim* to viii. 11).

It will not be necessary to give further examples of this type of exegesis, which exist in enormous quantities, for there is a great sameness about them; those cited will give a sufficiently clear idea regarding this point.

[1] *Cp.* the Midrash on Deuteronomy *Debarim Rabba*, ch. viii., where it is said: "As oil giveth light to the world, so do the words of the Tôrah give light to the world."

§ III. *Some examples of Messianic interpretation.*

Psalm ii. 1, 2: The "raging of the Gentiles" is interpreted as referring to the war of Gog and Magog (*Midr. T.*). One of the most important episodes in the eschatological drama is the great final conflict with the forces of the heathen nations ranged under Gog and Magog (see Ezek. xxxviii., xxxix.); a reference is made to this war in Rev. xvi. 14, and Gog and Magog are mentioned in Rev. xx. 7-10. In *Midr. T.*, where this passage is commented upon, it is said that David foresaw that Gog and Magog, together with their hosts, would fall before the Israelites, and he therefore cried: "Why do the nations rage . . ." *i.e.*, it was a futile proceeding on their part. In reference to v. 2, "The kings of the earth set themselves . . ." it is said, "When they (*i.e.* the enemies) shall realise their dire distress they will come and throw themselves at the feet of King Messiah." (See also p. 217 below.)

Psalm ii. 7: "Thou art my Son, this day have I begotten thee." In *Midr. T.* a rather subtle argument is used with the object, presumably, of combating Christian teaching. It is pointed out that the Hebrew for "Thou art my son" is *Beni attah*, *i.e.*, "My son art thou," but not *Ben li*, *i.e.*, "My son"; the point is that the former can be used of the relationship between master and disciple, etc., while the latter is specifically used of a man's son in the ordinary sense.

The text is, therefore, explained by saying; "It is as when a master, desirous of giving comfort and encouragement to his servant, says, "Thou art as dear to me as a son." Further, the words; "This day have I begotten thee," are explained by saying that after the period of woes and persecutions, which is to precede the Messianic era, is over, God will make a *new Creation* (*cp.* 2 Peter iii. 13: "But according to His promise we look for new heavens and a new earth"; see also Rev. xxi. 1-5). In Acts xiii. 33, the words under consideration are interpreted as referring to the resurrection of Christ; to them are added in verse 35 the quotation, "Thou wilt not give thy Holy One to see corruption" (Psalm xvi. 10, see further on this verse below). The Messianic interpretation of our passage is further emphasized in that it is compared with Dan. vii. 13: "Behold there came with the clouds of heaven one like unto the Son of Man" (cp. *Book of Enoch* lxii. 3 ff.); and a reference is also made to Ex. iv. 22, Isa. lii. 13, Psalm cx. 1, which should be consulted,

Psalm xviii. 49: "Therefore will I give thanks unto thee, O Lord, among the nations, and will sing praises unto Thy name."

St. Paul (Rom. xv. 9) quotes this in reference to the conversion of the Gentiles, but in *Midr. T.* it is regarded as a Messianic prophecy. It is there said that at the gathering of the exiled Israelites

David will give thanks unto the Lord among the nations; this is a reference to one of the great episodes of the Messianic Drama, viz. the Ingathering of Israel, to which reference is made in Isaiah xxvii. 13, (*cp.* Isaiah xlix. 22, lx. 4, 9, lxvi. 20), where it is anticipated that the Gentiles will themselves escort the exiles back. Passages like these exercised a great influence on the later ideas concerning the Messianic era; the exaltation of Israel in the presence of the heathen was to enhance the spiritual supremacy of the Israelites (see further Tobit xiii. 13, xiv. 5, Ecclus. xxxvi. 11, Psalms of Solomon xi. xvii., and *cp.* in the "Eighteen Blessings," or *Shemoneh Esreh* in the Jewish Liturgy the following: "Sound the great horn for our freedom; lift up the ensign to gather our exiles, and gather us from the four corners of the earth"). That in *Midr. T.* the verse before us is interpreted Messianically is further seen by the comment on the words, "And will sing praises unto Thy name," which says that this will be done "at the Advent of the Messiah."

Psalm xxix. 9: "And in His temple everything saith, Glory."

In the comment on these words in *Midr. T.* it is said that when the Messiah shall come He will immediately rebuild the sanctuary. One great hope associated with the coming of the Messiah was this rebuilding of the Temple; such prophecies as Ezek.

xl.-xliv., xlvii., Isa. liv. ii. ff., lx. 10 ff., which suggest the prospect of a new and glorious city, and a restored Temple-worship, strongly fostered such hopes. In Haggai ii. 7-9, the consciousness that the second Temple (before its restoration by Herod) compared unfavourably with the first is already apparent (*cp.* Tobit xiv. 5). It was expected that a new and glorious Jerusalem, of which the central point of beauty would of course be the Temple, would be built in the Messianic Age; this would glisten with sapphire, gold, and precious stones, etc. (*cp.* Tobit xiii. 15 ff., xiv. 4, Rev. xxi. 9-21). In later times, after the complete destruction of both city and Temple, this hope came to even more vivid expression. The restoration of the Holy City, and especially of the Temple-worship, long continued to be an object of pious hopes and prayers. Even at the present day the following is used in the *Shemoneh Esreh* of the Jewish Liturgy: "And to Jerusalem, thy city, return in mercy, and dwell therein, as Thou hast spoken; rebuild it soon in our days . . . Restore the service to the oracle of thy House, and receive in love and favour both the fire-offerings of Israel and their prayer; and may the service of Thy people Israel be ever acceptable unto Thee. And let our eyes behold Thy return in mercy to Zion."

Psalm lxxii. 17: "His name shall endure for ever . . ." This verse is Messianically interpreted in a number of Rabbinical writings, *e.g.*, according to *Bere-*

shith Rabba to i. 1.,[1] Rabbi Tanchuma taught that the Messiah was not actually created before the world, like the Torah and the Throne of Glory, but that his Name abode in the conception of the Creator[2] from times eternal. This verse is cited in support. The "name" here mentioned is, therefore, interpreted as referring to that of the Messiah.

Psalm lxxxvii. 4, 5: "I will make mention of Rabab and Babylon . . ."

This is explained in *Midr. T.* as referring to the time when all the nations will bring presents to King Messiah. On the words of verse 5, "Yea, of Zion it shall be said, This one and that one was born in her," the following comment is made: "These are the anointed ones of the Eternal, namely, the Messiah the son of David, and the Messiah the son of Ephraim." This "Messiah, the son of Ephraim," is the same as the "Messiah, the son of Joseph," referred to in Rabbinical apocalyptic literature. The earliest mention of him is in *Sukkah* 52 *a b* (Babylonian Talmud)[3] where three statements occur in regard to him, for the first of which Rabbi Dosa (*circa* 250 A.D.) is given as the authority. In the last of these statements only his name is mentioned, but the first two

[1] The *Midrash Pesikta* 54 *a*, and the Babylonian Talmud, *Nedarim* 39 *a*, are also referred to in the *Jewish Encycl.*, viii. 54 *a*; Weber, *Op. cit.* p. 355, refers also to the *Midrash* to *Proverbs* 67 *c*.

[2] The same is said in *Midr. T.* to xc. 2, xciii. 2.

[3] *Cp.* Weber, *Op. cit.*, p. 357.

speak of the fate which he is to meet, namely, to fall in battle (as if alluding to a well-known tradition). Details about him are not found until much later, but he has an established place in the apocalypses of later centuries and in the Midrashic literature. According to these, Messiah ben Joseph will appear prior to the coming of Messiah ben David; he will gather the children of Israel round him, march to Jerusalem, and there, after overcoming the hostile powers, re-establish the Temple-worship and set up his own dominion. Thereupon *Armilus*, according to one group of sources, or Gog and Magog, according to the other, will appear with their hosts before Jerusalem, wage war against Messiah ben Joseph, and slay him. His corpse, according to one group, will lie unburied in the streets of Jerusalem; according to the other, it will be hidden by the angels with the bodies of the Patriarchs, until Messiah ben David comes and resurrects him. When and how this Messiah-conception originated is a question that has not yet been answered satisfactorily. It is not possible to consider Messiah ben Joseph as the Messiah of the Ten Tribes; he is nowhere represented as such; it is mentioned that a part of the Ten Tribes will be found among those who will gather about his standard.

Psalm cx. 1. "The Lord said unto my Lord, Sit thou at my right hand, until I make thine enemies thy footstool."

(Quoted in Matt. xxii. 44, Mark xii. 36, Luke xix. 42, Heb. i. 13, *cp.* Heb. x. 13.) In *Midr. T.* these words are explained as referring to the Messiah. Reference is made to Isa. xvi. 5: "And a throne shall he establish in mercy, and one shall sit thereon in truth, in the tent of David." It then continues: "The Holy One, Blessed be He, said, 'Let him sit (on the throne), and I will wage the war.' And what has he (the Messiah) to do? He has to read and learn the *Torah*, which is called 'Truth,' as it is said, 'The judgements of the Lord are Truth' (Psalm xix. 10), and 'Buy the Truth and sell it not' (Prov. xxiii. 23). That is the meaning of the words: *One shall sit thereon in Truth.*"

In the *Yalkut Shimeoni*, it is said on this verse: "In time to come God will cause the Messiah to sit at His right hand, as it is written, *The Lord said, etc.*: but Abraham will sit at his left hand. Then Abraham's face will grow pale with shame, and he will say: 'The son of my son sits at thy right hand, and I sit at thy left.' But God will comfort him by saying: 'The son of thy son sits at My right hand, but I sit at *thy* right hand.'"[1]

§ IV. *Some Passages from the Psalms quoted in the New Testament.*

The *Jewish* use of the psalms quoted in the New Testament makes it a matter of interest to have some idea of the traditional exegesis on the passages there

[1] Quoted by Weber, *Op. cit.* p. 357.

quoted; for the most part the comments are disappointing, though some of them are worth considering.

Psalm ii. 1, 2. "Why do the nations rage and the peoples imagine a vain thing? The kings of the earth set themselves, and the rulers take counsel together against the Lord and against His anointed." (Quoted in Acts iv. 25, 26.)

Among those who "rage" are mentioned Pharaoh, Sisera, Sennacherib, and Nebuchadnezzar (*Midr. T.*), who set themselves against Jehovah. In the Acts, those who "rage" are Herod and Pilate (iv. 27); the *method* of exegesis is the same as in *Midr. T.* The "anointed" is not interpreted of the Messiah as in the New Testament (See also on this passage p. 210 above.)

Psalm ii. 7. "Thou art my Son, this day have I begotten thee."

(Quoted in Acts xiii. 33., Heb. i. 5). See above page 210 f.

Psalm viii. 2. "Out of the mouths of babes and sucklings hast thou established strength."

(Quoted in Matt. xxi. 16, where "strength" is rendered "praise," following the Septuagint.) The explanation of this verse given in *Midr. T.* is so extraordinary that it is worth while giving the passage in full. At the time of the giving of the Law on Mount Sinai, it is said, God required some pledge that the Israelites would keep the Law He was about to give them. Hostages were brought, but the Almighty could not accept them as such because they were not innocent; upon the people asking who they could bring who were perfectly innocent, God replied: "Children." Then they brought the children who were in their mother's wombs, and who were at their mother's breasts; and they looked up at the Holy One, Blessed be He, through their mothers' wombs as through crystal. Then the Holy One, Blessed be He, said unto them: "Will ye stand surety for your fathers, that they will keep the Law if I give it to them; and if they keep it not, will ye offer yourselves to be taken in their stead?" And they replied: "Yes." Then God recited all the commandments and asked the children if they would keep them; the promise having been given, He said, "It is because of this, your declaration, that I give the Law to them (your fathers)." Thus it came about that out of the mouths of babes and sucklings God established strength; for by strength is meant nothing else than the Law; as it is said in Psalm xxix. 11, "The Lord will give strength unto His people."

Psalm viii. 4-6. "What is man that thou art mindful of him . . ."

(Quoted in Heb. ii. 6-8.) On this passage see p. 200 above.

Psalm viii. 6. "Thou hast put all things under his feet."

(Quoted in 1 Cor. xv. 27, in reference to Christ.) In *Midr. T.* the reference is said to be to David.

Psalm xvi. 8-11. "I have set the Lord always before me. . . ."

(Quoted in Acts ii. 25-28, where the Septuagint is followed, and where it is given as a prophecy of David concerning Christ.)

The comments which are of interest commence with the words on, "Therefore my heart is glad;" in *Midr. T.* it is said that David's heart was glad concerning the words of the Law, and when he says, further, "My Glory rejoiceth," the reference is, according to Rabbinical interpretation, to his joy at the Messiah who will one day spring from his line. The words, "For thou wilt not leave my soul to Sheol . . ." are all taken to mean a reference of David to himself. Rabbi Isaac comments on the verse by saying that it proves that "the worm and corruption have had no power over his (*i.e.* David's) flesh"; contrast with this Acts xiii. 36, 37.

Psalm xxii. 1. "My God, my God, why hast thou forsaken me?"

(Quoted in Matt. xxvii. 46, Mark xv. 34.) In *Midr. T.* various interpretations, all more or less artificial, are given of these words; in one case it is said to have been uttered by the Israelites at the Red Sea; in another it is referred to Esther, possibly Esth. iv. 16 ("And if I perish, I perish") being in the mind of the writer; in the comments on several verses of this psalm the story of Esther is referred to.

Psalm xxii. 18. "They part my garments among them."

(Quoted in Matt. xxvii. 35, John xix. 24). In *Midr. T.* these words are explained by a reference to the downfall of Haman; they cast lots upon his vesture (which was of purple, according to Rabbi Huna) "because a common man could not make use of it."

Psalm xxiv. 1. "The earth is the Lord's, and the fulness thereof."

(Quoted in 1 Cor. x. 26, to show the lawfulness of eating all food.) In the comment on these words in *Midr. T.* there seems to be a covert attempt at refuting the Christian doctrine of the Logos as contained in John i. 1-3. It is said: "All are agreed that the angels were not created on the first day (of Creation),[1] that the heretics may not say, 'Michael worked (*lit.* spread out) from the East and Gabriel from the West, and the Holy One, blessed be He, created (*lit.* measured) in the centre,' for the Holy One, Blessed be He, created everything alone, as it is written, 'I am the Lord that maketh all things, that stretcheth forth the heavens above, that spreadeth abroad the earth, who is with me?' (Isa. xliv. 24); therefore David spoke in the

[1] In *Bereshith Rabba*, c. I., where this passage also occurs, it says: "Nothing, excepting the angels, was created on the first day."

presence of the Holy One, blessed be He, 'Because Thou didst create heaven and earth, therefore do I call them after Thy name, the earth is the Lord's, and the fulness thereof.'"

Psalm xxxii. 1, 2. "Blessed is he whose transgression is forgiven, whose sin is covered. Blessed is the man unto whom the Lord imputeth not iniquity."

(Quoted in Rom. iv. 7, 8, according to the Septuagint rendering.) St. Paul quotes these words in support of the doctrine of grace, "God reckoneth righteousness apart from works"; the reverse is the teaching given in *Midr. T.*, for it says there: "If a man offers (*lit.* does) genuine (*lit.* full) repentance, so that his heart is 'up-rooted,' the Holy One, Blessed be He, forgives him"; later on, the sense of these words comes out clearer, for it is said that the man is "blessed" because he has fulfilled a commandment of the Law, viz. that of showing repentance. The difference between the Jewish and the Christian doctrine lies here; according to the former, "the accomplishment of *Mitzvoth* (*i.e.* legal observances, *lit.* commandments), constitutes a meritorious act, and compels, as it were, divine approbation; they are *per se* the actual means of reconciliation, they are the *cause* whereby a right relationship, an at-one-ment between God and men, is established. According to Christian teaching Almsgiving, Repentance, etc., are also necessary, very indispensable, but there is nothing meritorious about them, their being left undone constitutes a sin which, as a sin, stands in the same category as sins of commission: 'When ye shall have done all things that are commanded you, say, we are unprofitable servants; we have done that which it was our duty to do,' *i.e.* nothing more than that. According to Christian teaching, no amount of simply doing what it is our duty to do could *per se* effect a right relationship with God, or could bring about justification."[1]

Psalm xli. 9. "Yea mine own familiar friend, in whom I trusted, which did eat of my bread, hath lifted up his heel against me."

(Quoted in part in John xiii. 18.) In *Midr. T.* these words are interpreted as referring to a teacher and his pupils: "When they go before into the house of learning, they enter like gentle kids; but when they go out before me they are like goats who butt with their horns." The word "heel" is said to mean "end," in reference to the end of the time of instruction.

Psalm li. 4. "Against thee only have I sinned . . that thou mayest be justified when thou speakest, and be clear when thou art judged."

(Quoted in part of Rom. iii. 14, following the Septuagint.) The comment in *Midr. T.* on this verse is as follows: "With whom is David here to be compared? With one who had broken (a limb), and who came to the physician. The physician gazed in

[1] Oesterley, *The Jewish Doctrine of Mediation*, pp. 199 f. (1910).

wonderment, and said, 'How great is thy hurt? I am in fear concerning thee.' Then he with the broken limb answered, 'Thou art in fear on my account! But I only broke it for the sake of thy fee.' Thus also did David speak unto the Holy One, Blessed be He: 'Against Thee only have I sinned, when Thou sayest to the evil-doers, wherefore do ye not show forth repentance? For if Thou receivest me, then all the evil-doers will be reconciled with Thee (*lit.* will submit themselves to Thee), and will all look upon me; for I act as witness that Thou dost receive all who are repentant.' For thus saith the Holy One, Blessed be He, 'Behold, I have given him for a witness to the people' (Isa. lv. 4), and not only I, but all Israel, acts as witness, for it is said, 'Ye are My witnesses, saith the Lord, and My servant whom I have chosen'" (Isa. xliii. 10). The passage is of great interest, as it seems to imply a belief in the doctrine of vicarious atonement.

Psalm lxviii. 18. "Thou hast ascended on high, Thou hast led Thy captivity captive, Thou hast received gifts among men."

(Quoted freely in Eph. iv. 8, in reference to the Ascension.) In *Midr. T.* it is explained in reference to Moses, when he ascended up to Mount Sinai (Exod. xix. 3). The "gifts" are said to refer to the Law.

Psalm lxxviii. 2. "I will open my mouth in a parable, I will utter dark sayings of old.,'

(Quoted in Matt. xiii. 36, from the Septuagint.) In

Midr. T. the verse is explained by the words in Prov. i. 6, and is said to refer to the words of the Law. According to Rabbinical teaching the Tôrah existed before the world was created (*cp.* the Midrash *Shemoth Rabba*, c. 33).

Psalm lxxviii. 24, 25. "And gave them of the corn of heaven; man did eat the bread of the mighty." (Quoted, in substance, in John vi. 31.) The only comment of interest in *Midr. T.* is on the words, "bread of the mighty"; they received this bread, it is said, because they had become mighty as the angels. It is not called "angels' food," as the Prayer Book Version renders it, but food fit for mighty men.

Psalm xci. 11, 12. "For He shall give his angels charge over thee, to keep thee in all thy ways. They shall bear thee up in their hands, lest thou dash thy foot against a stone." (Quoted in Matt. iv. 6, freely, in Luke iv. 10, 11, more accurately.)

In *Midr. T.* it is said, "Who is greater, he that beareth, or he that is borne? Answer: He that is borne." The implication is, that Jacob, in reference to whom the passage is explained, was greater than the angels. In the context of this passage in the Gospel, it is said: "Then the devil taketh him into the Holy City, and setteth him on the pinnacle of the temple. . . ." In view of these words it is interesting to notice the further comment given in *Midr.* T.: "Our Rabbis taught thus: The smallest possible number of stones (conceivable) is two; but when Jacob awoke in the morning he found that they had become one, and great fear overcame him, and he said: The house of the Holy One, Blessed be He, is at this spot, and I knew not that it was his dwelling-place, as it is written in Gen. xxviii. 17, 'How dreadful is this place. . .' Hence our Rabbis taught: To everyone who prays in Jerusalem, it is reckoned as though he had prayed before the throne of glory, for the gate of Heaven is there, and the door stands open, that prayer may be heard, as it is written,—'This is none other than the gate of Heaven.' And Jacob returned in order to gather the stones, but he found that they had become one stone, and he took this stone and set it up as a pillar in the centre of that place; and oil flowed down from Heaven, which he took and poured upon the stone—as it is written (Gen. xxviii. 18). Then what did the Holy One, Blessed be He, do? With His right foot he trod upon the stone so that it sank deep down into the earth. Therefore it is called 'The Foundation Stone,' for there is the central point of the earth, and thereon stands the Temple of the Eternal One, as it is written, 'And this stone which I have set up for a pillar shall be God's house' (Gen. xxviii. 22). And Jacob fell upon his face upon the earth before the Foundation Stone."

Psalm xciv. 14; "For the Lord will not cast off His people." (Quoted in Rom. xi. 2, from the Septuagint.)

The comment in *Midr. T.* on this passage is: "Our Rabbis teach that God does not cast off those who live outside the Holy Land (*i.e.*, the Jews of the Dispersion) because of His great name; those who live in the land of Israel He does not cast off because they are His people and His inheritance." Another comment is worth quoting, because it teaches the doctrine of grace apart from works: "God does not cast off the Israelites when they do His will, because they are His people and His inheritance; but even when they are wanting in good works He does not cast them off, for His great Name's sake."

Psalm civ. 4: "Who maketh winds his messengers, his ministers a flaming fire." (Quoted in Heb. i. 7.)

In *Midr. T.* we have the following comment: "Rabbi Jochanan taught, 'The angels were created on the second day. Those who are employed as messengers are (created) out of wind. . . . but those who are employed as ministers are (created) out of fire.'"

Psalm cxvii. 1: "O praise the Lord, all ye nations, laud Him all ye peoples." (Quoted in Rom. xv. 11, in reference to the conversion of the Gentiles.)

In *Midr. T.* a variety of curious comments are given on this verse, various authorities being cited. The only comment which bears any direct relationship to the words of the text is that of Rabbi Simeon; this is as follows: "Rabbi Simeon, the son of our holy teacher, asked his father, 'Who are all the *nations*, and who are all the *peoples?*' He answered, 'All the *nations* are such as have been subjugated by the Israelites, and all the *peoples* are such as have not been subjugated by the Israelites.' All the *peoples* say, 'If all the *nations*, who are subject to the children of Israel, praise the Holy One, Blessed be He, how much more ought we, who are not subject to them, to praise Him.' Therefore it is written, 'O praise the Lord, all ye nations, laud Him all ye peoples.' And the Israelites said, 'How much more ought we to do the same.'"

This passage is interesting on account of its universalistic tendency, a tendency which is, generally speaking, more characteristic of the prophetical than of the Rabbinical writings. It is well to remember that St. Paul, in his attitude towards the Gentiles, was wholly supported by one type of Judaism.

Psalm cxviii. 6: "The Lord is on my side, I will not fear what man can do unto me." (Quoted in Heb. xiii. 6.)

In *Midr. T.* this is illustrated thus: "Abraham said, 'The Eternal One is with me, I fear not; what can Nimrod do unto me?' Isaac said, 'The Eternal One is with me, I fear not; what can Abimelech do unto me?' Jacob said, 'The Eternal One is with me, I fear not; what can Esau and Laban do unto me?' In the same way David said, 'The Lord is with me, I fear not; what can Goliath do unto me?'"

Psalm cxviii. 22, 23: The stone which the builders

rejected is become the head of the corner. This is the Lord's doing; it is marvellous in our eyes." (Quoted in Matt. xxi. 42; Mark xii. 10, 11; Luke xx. 17; *cp.* Acts iv. 11.)

In *Midr. T.* attention is drawn to the fact that part of the seed of both Abraham and Isaac (viz. Ishmael and all the sons of Keturah, and Esau) was rejected, but that the seed of Jacob consisted of the twelve tribes, who were perfect. In reference to this seed Cant. iv. 7, is quoted; "Thou art all fair, my love; and there is no spot in thee." In the Midrash *Shir ha-Shirim* these words are illustrated by a reference to Jacob.

Regarding verse 23 above it is said in *Midr. T.* that it refers to David: "He was feeding his father's flocks, and within a short hour he had become king; and all (the people) said, 'Just now he was a shepherd, yet now he is a king.' He answered them, 'Ye marvel concerning me, but I marvel concerning myself more than ye do.' Then the Holy Spirit uttered the words, 'This is the Lord's doing.'"

Psalm cxviii. 26: "Blessed is he that cometh in the name of the Lord." (Quoted in Mark xi. 9.)

In *Midr. T.* it is merely said that these words were uttered by the men of Jerusalem in reference to the "Holy One of Israel," spoken of in Isa. xii. 6.

The instances of the Jewish exegesis of the Psalms here offered may be said to give a fair general idea of the subject; they bear out the conclusion which is forced upon one after a considerable study of this branch of Jewish exegesis, namely that so far as any real elucidation of the text is concerned, but little help is to be gained. Its use is to be found rather in another direction; for, from the examples given, it will have been noticed that quite a number of the comments throw light upon, or illustrate, *doctrinal subjects*; it is in this domain that the traditional exegesis is frequently of real value; and this it is which makes it worth while to give attention to the subject.

CHAPTER XII.

A COMMENTARY ON PSALM XCI.

A SOMEWHAT close investigation of this psalm reveals the fact that it was probably originally written for a purpose which at first sight is not apparent. It has always occupied an important place among the Jews, both privately as well as in public worship (see Chapter IX.); an examination of it here will, therefore, not be out of place. The translation to be given is a literal one, sometimes based on an emendation of the Hebrew text.

In Rabbinical literature this psalm is called "a song for evil encounters,"[1] and its use in the event of demoniacal onslaughts is recommended. There must have been something particularly appropriate about the psalm to have occasioned such a recommendation. Its late date,[2] certainly post-exilic, is a fact of importance from the point of view of our present investigation, for

[1] *E.g.*, *Shebuoth*, 15 *b* (Babylonian Talmud).

[2] *Cp.* Briggs, *Psalms* (Internat. Crit. Com.), I, pp. xc., xci., who assigns it to the "Early Greek" period.

the influence of Babylonian thought upon the exiles was, it is well known, very marked; and it is in the highest degree probable that this influence was as strong in the domain of popular demonology as in any other direction. There is reason to believe[1] that from the earliest times the Israelites had an extensive demonology, of a popular kind, which was the common property of the Semitic race; so that when Babylonian influence began once more,[2] during the Exile, to be exercised upon the captives, there was very probably a fertile soil ready to receive any new seed which eastern winds might blow towards it. This, added to the fact that the thoroughly established Monotheism of post-exilic times had to a great extent eliminated the danger of demon-cults, would mainly account for the more fully developed and officially recognised demonology of later Judaism.[3]

Now one of the most marked characteristics of all systems of demonology is the use of formulas, incantations and the like, for the purpose of counteracting, or rendering nugatory, the evil machinations of demons; the number of Babylonian "magic" texts for exorcising demons that have been recovered is very large.[4]

[1] See the writer's article, "The Demonology of the Old Testament," in the *Expositor* for April, 1907, pp. 318 ff.

[2] It will be remembered that in much earlier times Babylonian influence as is proved by the Tell-el-Amarna tablets, had been immense.

[3] Persia and Greece, of course, also contributed their quota; see the articles by F. C. Conybeare in the *Jewish Quarterly Review*, vols. viii. ix. (1896, 1897).

[4] See M. Jastrow, *Die Religion Babyloniens und Assyriens*, chap xvi.

One or two extracts from these will not be inappropriate here. The following is addressed to a demon :—

> As long as thou dost not stir from the body of the man, the son of his god, as long as thou dost not budge, thou shalt eat no food neither drink water; the goblet of Bel, the father that bore thee, shalt thou not touch with thy hand, neither shalt thou be covered with water from the sea, nor with sweet water, nor with bitter water, nor with water from the Tigris, nor with water from the Euphrates, nor with well-water, nor with water from a river. When thou desirest to fly to the heavens thy wings will refuse (their office) . . .[1]

Or again :

> I call upon you, ye gods of the night, with you I call upon the night, the veiled bride, I call at eventide, at midnight, at early dawn.[2]

The Jews also had various means of exorcising demons ; among others was that recommended by Rashi : "If a demon hears his name pronounced (repeatedly), each time with a syllable less, he will flee" ; an example which he gives is the name of the demon Shabiri, which had to be called out thus :—

Shabiri, abiri, biri, ri.[3]

Another formula was : "The Lord rebuke thee" (*cp.* Zech. iii. 2).

[1] O. Weber, *Dämonenbeschwörung bei den Babyloniern und Assyriern*, in "Der alte Orient," vii. 4.

[2] M. Jastrow, *Op. cit.* p. 287. For a Greek example, see Deissmann, *Bibelstudien* 28 ff.

[3] F. Weber, *Jüdische Theologie auf Grund des Talmud und verwandter Schriften*, p. 257.

Under Babylonian influence, it can scarcely be doubted, many formulas were used by the Jews for the purpose of driving away demons; this was, however, as we shall see, not by any means the only method of combating them, for, on Arabian and Babylonian analogy,[1] it is permissible to infer that there were certain classes of both men and women to whom recourse was had for helping the victims of what were believed to be demoniacal onslaughts.

The theory, then, with regard to the ninety-first Psalm, which the following pages will attempt to justify, is that it is a polemic, in devotional form, against current methods of securing oneself against demons. The Psalmist undoubtedly believed in demons and their works; his ideas regarding them were in agreement—so the psalm itself seems to teach—with the popular beliefs of his day; where he disagreed *in toto* from these was in the methods which were supposed to be efficacious in shielding oneself from the malicious activity of the demons. Not in formulas and enchantments, not by means of wizards and witches, but only with the help, and under the protection, of Jehovah was there any real security from the curse of demons.

Verse 1. *He that abideth under the protection of the Most High, passes the night in the shadow of Shaddai.*

The point of importance here is that the root of the

[1] See the writer's article, "The Demonology of the Old Testament, illustrated from the Prophetical Writings," in the *Expositor* for June 1907, pp. 535 ff.

[2] Wellhausen, *Reste Arabischen Heidenthums* (2. ed.), p. 151.

word rendered "abide" in the Revised Version means "to pass the night" (*cp.* Genesis xix. 2, Judges xix. 13, 14, 2 Samuel xvii. 16). Now, it was especially at night-time that the demons' power was supposed to be greatest, and consequently their activity most pronounced. The Arabs believed that after dark was the time during which demons were about, and that their activity continued until the morning-star rose.[1] The Babylonians said, for example, that the "Wicked Seven" were so powerful at nights that they were even able to oppress the moon, until the rising sun came to her help.[2] In a Babylonian hymn it is said that the rising sun drives away all evil spirits.[3] Another hymn describes how Shamash, the Sun-god, proceeds at morn from the great mountain of the east, and bans with his bright rays all the murky demons who frolic during the hours of darkness. So, too, in Rabbinical literature; the solitary wanderer at night is in special danger of demons,[4] and, according to the Midrash *Bereshith Rabba*, c. 36, the time for demons is from dusk till cock-crowing. During this time they will surround a house and harm anyone who comes out; and they will kill children who are out after dark.[5]

It is possible that in the phrase "in the shadow of Shaddai" there is a covert reference to the "darkness

[1] Wellhausen, *Reste Arabischen Heidenthums*, p. 151.

[2] O Weber, *Op. cit.* p. 10.

[3] Jeremias, *Das A.T. im Lichte des alten Orients*, pp. 35, 342.

[4] *Pesachim*, 112*b*. (Babylonian Talmud).

[5] F Weber, *Op. cit.* p. 255.

of Shaddai (the Almighty), "*i.e.* the darkness wherein, according to the true believer, *Jehovah* is all-powerful, as contrasted with the darkness of the demons, *i.e.* the darkness wherein, according to the popular fallacy, the demons are supreme; at all events, the root idea of the Hebrew word for "shadow" (*i.e.* shade) is "to be dark." Then, again, it is perhaps not fanciful to see in "Shaddai" a word-play; one of the most prominent figures in Babylonian demonology was the bull-shaped *Shedu;* in Jewish demonology one of the main categories into which demons are divided is that of the *Shedim*, whose leader is Asmedai (Asmodeus, *cp.* Tobit iii. 8, 17); they exist in great numbers, they have wings, and are active at nights, especially in the wilderness, though their presence is not confined to the desert. According to one account, they were originally serpents, and by a process of evolution became *Shedim* (*Baba Kamma, Babylonian Talmud*, 16*a*).[1] It is, therefore, possible that in "Shaddai" a word-play was intended. It is, of course, not suggested that there is any radical connexion between *Shaddai* and *Shedim;* similarity of sound was quite sufficient for those word-plays which so frequently occur in the biblical books.

Verse 2. *That saith*[2] *to Jehovah, My refuge and my defence, my God; in Him do I trust.*

The stress is laid here on *Jehovah*, because it was just

[1] F. Weber, *Op. cit.* p. 254.

[2] So the *Septuagint;* the opening word of the psalm, "he that abideth" presupposes some word like "Blessed (is the man that)," which very likely preceded it originally; *cp.* Psalm i. 1.

this trust in *Him* that formed the contrast to the popular method of securing oneself against demons. These popular methods have already been referred to; but some little detail is necessary here. Among the Babylonians there was a regular class of priests called "mash-mashu,"[1] whose special calling it was to ban demons when they had taken possession of a man, or were injuring him in any way. It was to these priests that men fled for refuge and defence in their terror, believing that the ban-formula or incantation which the priests prescribed was all-sufficient. Nor are we without definite proof that something of the same kind existed among the Jews. The following passages will show this: in Isa. xlvii. 9, 12, in the first place, we read of sorceries and enchantments prevalent among the Babylonians, showing that these methods were known of in Palestine; but that they were, indeed, also prevalent among the Israelites both before and after the Exile is clear from these passages: Micah v. 12 (11 in Hebrew): "And I will cut off witchcrafts out of thine hand; and thou shalt have no more soothsayers"; Deut. xviii. 10, 11: "There shall not be found with thee . . . one that useth divination, one that practiseth augury, or an enchanter, or a sorcerer, or a charmer, or a consulter with a familiar spirit, or a wizard, or a necromancer"; Jer. xxvii. 9: "Hearken ye not to your prophets, nor to your diviners, nor to your dreams, nor to your soothsayers, nor to your sorcerers . . .;"

[1] O. Weber, *Op. cit.* p. 7.

cp. also Nahum iii. 4; Num. xxiii. 23, xxiv. 1; Malachi iii. 5; Wisdom xii. 4-6. It is, therefore, extremely likely that there was much the same practice in Judæa as in Babylonia; namely, that there was a class of men (priests), to whom people went for help when attacked, as they supposed, by demons. If this is so, then the verse before us may well have been the Psalmist's expression of the blessedness of those who, like himself, looked to Jehovah for help and defence, instead of to the men in whom his less enlightened fellows trusted when assailed by evil powers.

Verse 3. *For He shall deliver thee from the net of the fowler.*

The emphatic "He" recalls what was said above about the emphasis on *Jehovah.* It must be confessed that it is not altogether easy to see where the danger lies for *men* in a fowler's net; the word in the original means only a small net, it was not like the *resheth* which was a large net spread over the ground (*cp.* Psalms ix. 15); generally speaking, however, it is used figuratively of the plots or evil machinations of men, but in the whole passage there is little or nothing to show that the evils from which protection is given, are the works of evil-disposed men. The parallel clause of this verse speaks of the "noisome pestilence" (though on this, see below), and later on there is mention of "the terror by night," "the arrow that flieth by day," the "pestilence that walketh in darkness," "the destruction that wasteth at noonday," and so on throughout the psalm; these (even the "arrow" that flieth by day, see below) are all things very far removed from anything in the shape of plots, or the like, on the part of *men;* the one exception is verse eight, which speaks of "the reward of the wicked," but it will be allowed that the psalm reads equally smoothly if this verse is omitted; according to the interpretation of the psalm here offered, verse eight did not belong to it in its original form, because it disturbs the context. But whether the interpretation is right or wrong, it is interesting to see that Prof. Briggs, in his "Commentary,"[1] regards this verse as due to a glossator, though on quite different grounds from those here set forth. If, however, "net" in verse three, is used figuratively, and refers to some demoniacal craft, then its use is distinctly significant here; for in this connexion it is interesting to recall the fact that according to both Arabian and Babylonian belief there was a very close relationship between demons and witches. The Arabs held that witches were the incarnations of demons[2]; the Babylonians believed them to be just as dangerous as demons; indeed, according to Babylonian belief, the two were often in league with one another, and played into each other's hands, and both enchanters and witches had the power of impressing demons into their service. Death follows in the trail of a witch, so ran the belief; her eyes and feet and hands were all quicker and more mobile than

[1] Vol. ii. pp. 280 ff. [2] Wellhausen, *Op. cit.* p. 159.

those of ordinary men and women; like demons, the witches took up their abode in forsaken sites; when a witch spies a victim, the Babylonians taught, she follows him, entangles his feet in her net, and drags him to the ground.[1] Most of all she loves to be active at night-time; and she is known as the "Huntress of the night."[2]

It will be conceded that these facts are significant (see further below); for if these kinds of ideas were current at the time in Judæa as well as in Babylonia—and there is every reason to suppose that this was the case—then our Psalmist must have known of them, and they must have been in his mind when he wrote the psalm; that is to say, he was here thinking of the witch's net, in the use of which she was assisted by a demon.

From the destructive word (R.V. "From the noisome pestilence"). This rendering is based on the *Septuagint* version, all the great MSS. concurring, together with the Syriac version and that of Symmachus. It is true that this rendering does not, *at first sight*, suit the parallel clause, "the net of the fowler;" but this is true also of the Massoretic text as it stands. But possibly there is more justification for the *Septuagint* rendering than appears at first sight; at all events, according to the present method of interpreting the psalm, the Greek gives good sense and affords a

[1] These are the actual expressions.

[2] *Cp. Rabisu*, the "Lurker," who is an important figure in Babylonian demonology.

perfect parallel to the other clause of the verse. Just as there were certain classes of men to whom, as we have seen, people went when they believed themselves to be oppressed by a demon, and just as these men professed to break the power of demons by means of written formulas, magical incantations, charms and the like, so there were other classes, comprising both men and women, who were believed to be in league with demons, and who could harm people by using spells and practising certain unhallowed rites, whereby they forced demons to do an injury, to cause sickness, and even to bring about death. A close connexion, as we have seen, has always been believed to exist between demons and witches; these latter almost take up an intermediate position between human beings and demons in the Babylonian system. Professor Jastrow says: "No sharp distinction is made between the living magician or witch and the various demons who flit about like ghosts or carry on their machinations in invisible form . . . For this reason it happens that in the same adjuration a witch and a demon are addressed indiscriminately. And since one cannot know for a certainty which particular demon is at work, it is customary to name various categories of them. In the same way it may happen that the witch who is causing trouble is wholly unknown, and may be taking every means to remain so."[1] In such cases a form of adjuration is used which has a general application, whether in reference to demons

[1] *Op. cit.* p. 309.

generally, or witches in general, or to both (see the extract below). Difficult as it is for us to realize the fact, it is nevertheless important to remember that the beliefs regarding the power for harm that witches had constituted a terrible reality and must have been a constant source of fear and anxiety; one has only to read some of the immense numbers of magic texts, and the like, to realise how deeply people must have felt upon the subject, and what a terrible curse upon the community generally must have been the belief in these ubiquitous demons and their allies in human form. The following is an interesting example of a Babylonian adjuration pronounced against some unknown witch who was believed to be entangling her victim, with the help, of course, of a demon:

Who art thou, enchantress, that carries in her heart *the evil word* against me,
Upon whose tongue was destruction against me;
Through whose lips have I been poisoned,
In the train of whose footsteps follows death?
Enchantress, I grasp thy mouth, I grasp thy tongue,
I grasp thy piercing eyes,
I grasp thy ever mobile feet,
I grasp thy ever active knees,
I grasp thy ever outstretched hands,
I bind thy hands behind thee.
May Sin (*i.e.* the Moon-god) destroy thy body,
May he cast thee into an abyss of water and fire;
Enchantress, like the setting of this signet ring
May thy face glow and then grow pale.

The last line refers to the melting and getting cool

again of the gold.[1] It is clear enough from this typical extract that a spell was believed to have been pronounced, and that the adjuration was recited for the purposes of counteracting the evil effects of the *word* of occult magic. It is conceivable that in the verse before us the Psalmist was referring to something of this kind; its meaning would then be that Jehovah and nobody else, could deliver men from the magic spell ("word") of magician, witch or demon.

Verse 4. *With His pinions He covers thee, yea, under His wings thou findest refuge.*

The protective care of Jehovah is again emphasised; the thought of finding safety under His wings occurs several times in the Psalms (xvii. 8, xxxvi. 7, lxi., lxi. 4, lxiii. 7); it echoes, possibly, an ancient conception. Quite conceivably a covert contrast is intended between the protecting wings of Jehovah and those which some kinds of demons were believed to have; the demons used their wings to fly swiftly on their harmful errands, but under Jehovah's wings the terror-stricken would be safe.

A shield and a buckler is His truth (or "faithfulness").

The fact that the Psalmist uses figurative language suggests that the foes to be shielded against are not men, but spiritual enemies. In the Midrash to the Psalms one of the comments on these words runs: "Rabbi Simeon ben Jochai said, 'The weapon which the Holy One, Blessed be He, gave to the Israelites at Sinai was described

[1] *Ibid.* 309.

with the unutterable Name of God.'" The Holy One (pronounced Adonai) is elsewhere referred to as a means of safeguard against evil powers; thus, the reading of the *Shema*, because it contains the Name of God in the first verse, is recommended for this purpose (*Berachoth* 5 *a*, Babylonian Talmud); the priest's blessing, also because it mentions God's Name, is efficacious.

Verse 5. *Thou shalt not be afraid because of the night-terror or because of the arrow that flieth by day.*

To what does this "Night-terror" refer? In the Midrash to the Psalms we have this interesting comment: "Rabbi Berechja said, 'There is a harmful spirit that flies like a bird and shoots like an arrow.'" According to Jewish teaching, *Lilith*, the Night-hag, got her name from *Layilah*, "night"; the etymology was false, but that does not effect the belief that Lilith was the night-demon *par excellence*. The connexion was suggested by the similarity of the two words, as well as by the fact that Lilith was believed to be especially active at nights. On the assumption that Jewish belief in demons was profoundly influenced by that of Babylonia, it will be instructive to inquire as to the popular Babylonian belief concerning Lilith, especially as it is more than probable that she was worshipped by some of the Jewish exiles in Babylon[1]. A demon-triad is formed by Lilu, Lilitu, and Ardat Lili; the male, the female, and the handmaid; the

[1] See Levy, in the *Zeitschrift der Deutschen Morgenländischen Gesellschaft* ix. 470 ff.

Biblical Lilith would correspond to the second of these, Lilitu. These three are more particularly storm-demons, who rush about at night seeking what harm they can do to men; they are spoken of as flying, and were therefore most likely, though not necessarily, conceived of as having wings; Ardat Lili is once spoken of as "flitting in through a window" after a man; and she was believed to inflame evil passions; sleeplessness and nightmare were regarded as her handiwork.[1] A magical text which probably refers to Ardat Lili is quoted by Jastrow; it is so appropriate that part of it may be quoted here —

> "The entangler of those that entangle,
> The enchantress of those that enchant,
> Whose net lies spread out in the streets,
> Whose eyes peer about in the open spaces of the city,
> Among them am I, at whom she makes a dead set;
> She surrounds the maidens in the city,
> Among them am I . . .
> May thy evil mouth be filled with dust,
> May thy evil tongue be bound with thongs
> At the command of Marduk, the Lord of Life."[2]

That the demon Lilitu was not unknown in Israel is clear from Isaiah xxxiv. 14. But it is in the later Jewish beliefs, especially as found stereotyped in Rabbinical literature, that the importance of Lilith appears; for, as there is every reason to believe, this later literature reflects earlier thought. Here she

[1] M. Jastrow, *Op. cit.* pp. 278 ff.

[2] M. Jastrow, *Op. cit.* p. 319. An illustration of an Assyrian demon which may have been a representation of Lilitu is given in Jeremias, *Op. cit.* p. 342.

appears as the head of one of the three great classes into which the demons (*Mazzikin*—" Harm-doers ") are divided, viz. the *Lilin,* who take their name from her. They are of human shape, but they have wings ; they are all females ; children are the main objects of their wrath. Lilith is conceived of as a beautiful woman, with long flowing hair ;[1] she is dangerous to men,[2] and it is especially at nights, though not exclusively so, that she comes out to seek her victims. These few details will be sufficient for our purpose ; they certainly afford some grounds for the supposition that the "Night-terror" was this female demon, Lilith. This idea is strengthened by the fact that, according to Jewish tradition, the meteor-stone was called "the arrow of Lilith."

Verse 6. (*Or*) *because of the pestilence that goeth about in darkness.*

Here one is reminded of the well-known Babylonian pest-demon, Namtar. He is often spoken of as the "violent Namtar," and he comes as the pest-bringing envoy from the realms of the dead, like a "raging wind." The following short extract from one of the magical texts shows how he must have been feared :—

> "Terrible Namtar, strong Namtar. Namtar, who will not leave men ; Namtar, who will not go away ; Namtar, who will not depart ; wicked Namtar . . . "[3]

Significant, too, is the introduction to another text describing the action of this " Demon of pestilence " :—

[1] See, *e.g.*, M. Jastrow, *Op. cit.* p. 350.

[2] *Cp.* "Frau Holde" in Teutonic myth.

[3] M. Jastrow, *Op. cit.* p. 369.

"Wicked Namtar, who scorches the land like fire, who approaches a man like Asakku,[1] who rages through the wilderness like a storm-wind, who pounces upon a man like a robber, who plagues a man like the pestilence, who has no hands, no feet, who goes about at night . . . "[2]

Here, it cannot be denied, we have a forcible reminder of the very words of the psalm, "the pestilence that goeth about in darkness." That pestilence, and sickness of every kind, was due to the action of demons, was likewise believed by the Arabs; it was also the teaching of later Judaism.[3] The latter half of this verse is very instructive:—

(Or) because of Keteb and the mid-day demon.

This rendering will be explained in a moment. The word "Keteb," usually translated "destruction," only occurs elsewhere three times (Deut. xxxii. 24, Isa. xxviii. 2, Hos. xiii. 14), and in each case there are reasons for believing that the reference is to a demon. That in the verse before us the thought of a demon was present is certain if, as seems not improbable, the *Septuagint* and Aquila reflect a more original form than the present Hebrew text; in each of these there is a direct reference to a demon. In Rabbinical literature the verse was understood in this sense,[4] and *Keteb* is used there as the proper name of a demon

[1] Another Babylonian demon of great power for harm.

[2] O. Weber, *Op. cit.* p. 16.

[3] See the *Expositor* (April, 1907), p. 327, and *cp.* the many instances in the Gospels, *cp.* Hastings' *Dict. of Christ and the Gospels*, I. p. 441.

[4] *E.g. Pesachim*, 111 *b*, Babylonian Talmud.

(see below). It is for these reasons that the translation given above seems justified. That there should have been a belief in some special mid-day demon is highly probable; in later Judaism it was believed that demons were specially active then,[1] and in some Babylonian texts there are some suggestive passages.[2] The Midrash to the Psalms is so instructive on this verse that a short extract may be given; in reference to *Keteb* we read: "Our Rabbis said, 'It is a demon (*Shēd*)'"; the words that follow are unfortunately untranslatable, owing to the corrupt state of the text; but it continues; "Rabbi Huna, speaking in the name of Rabbi Jose, said; 'The poisonous *Keteb* was covered with scales and with hair, and sees only out of one eye, the other one is in the middle of his heart; and he is powerful, not in the darkness nor in the sun, but between darkness and the sun(shine). He rolls himself up like a ball and stalks about from the fourth to the ninth hour, from the 17th of Tammuz to the 9th of Ab; and everyone who sees him falls down on his face.' Rabbi Pinchas bar Chama, the priest, said, 'Once a man saw him, and he was thrown down upon his face.' Rabbi Samuel bar Rab Jizhak commanded the schoolmasters to let the children be free during those four hours. Rabbi Jochanan commanded the schoolmasters not to whip the children from the 17th of Tammuz to

[1] F. Weber, *Op. cit.* p. 254.

[2] M. Jastrow, *Op. cit.* pp. 332, 342-345.

the 9th of Ab. That is what the words, 'Because of Keteb, who destroys at mid-day,' mean."

Verse 7. *A thousand shall fall at thy side, and ten thousand at thy right hand, unto thee it shall not come nigh.*

There is no difficulty about either the Hebrew or Greek text here, they are in perfect order; the difficulty of the passage lies in the question as to what is the correct interpretation of it; what do the words refer to? It is, of course, possible to explain the "thousands" as referring to those who do not trust in Jehovah, these men will in consequence become victims of the pestilence spoken of in the preceding verse. This, however, seems to be pushing poetical licence a little too far, especially (as has already been pointed out) in view of the fact that there is little or nothing in the psalm to show that wicked men are referred to (see above, on verse 3). In accordance with the general belief in the existence of great numbers of demons, it seems permissible to hold that the "thousands" in this verse refer to these. The Arabs certainly believed that there were immense numbers of them;[1] this belief was shared by the Babylonians;[2] in a Babylonian text, moreover, reference is made to the demons who walk at the side of a man,[3] thus forcibly recalling the verse before us. The teaching of later Judaism agrees with this; in the Babylonian

[1] Wellhausen, *Op. cit.* pp. 148, 149.

[2] See further, *Expositor* (April, 1907), p. 325.

[3] M. Jastrow, *Op. cit.* pp. 355, 357.

Talmud, *Berachoth* 51*a*, it is said that the demons gather themselves together in companies; the whole world is full of *Mazzikin*, according to *Tanchuma Mishpatim* 19;[1] the number is given by one Rabbi as seven and a half millions; elsewhere it is stated that every man has ten thousand at his right hand and a thousand at his left—a clear indication, as it would seem, of the Rabbinical interpretation of our psalm. Moreover, in the Midrash to the Psalms this verse is commented on as follows: "The left hand . . . . a thousand angels protect, in order to guard it against evil spirits; the right hand . . . ten thousand angels protect, in order to guard it against evil spirits. Rabbi Chanina bar Abahu said: . . . If a thousand evil spirits assemble at thy left hand they fall . . . and if ten thousand assemble at thy right hand they fall . . ."

The meaning of this verse may, therefore, with some justification be said to be that although a man be surrounded by these thousands of invisible enemies, no harm will come to him if he puts his trust in Jehovah, because Jehovah's angels will protect him by annihilating them (see v. 11). The words, "unto thee it shall not come nigh," must then refer to the harm from which the man who trusts in Jehovah will be preserved.

Verse 8. As pointed out under verse 3, there are reasons for regarding this verse as a gloss.

Verse 9. *For* [*Thou Jehovah art my refuge*] *the Most High hast thou chosen as thy protector.*

[1] F. Weber, *Op. cit.*, p. 254.

The text here is obviously out of order[1]; the words which have been placed in square brackets are most likely a gloss. But the meaning of the verse is clear; the thousands of demons who assail a man cannot do him any injury if he looks to Jehovah as his protector. It will be seen that if verse eight and the words enclosed in brackets be deleted, the sequence of thought, as well as the actual text, runs more smoothly.

Verse 10. *No evil shall befall thee, neither shall any plague come nigh thy tent.*

The late Professor Curtiss, in his very interesting book *Primitive Semitic Religion To-Day*, remarks that the "modern Semite who has remained untouched by the world's progress may represent a primitive religion which was in existence before the ancient Babylonian empire began to be, or was even thought of"[2]; and later on in his book he gives, among many other illustrations, the following instances: "When the people go into the country to cultivate the soil, they often live in caves near the harvest-field. Before taking up their abode in the cave they offer a sacrifice to the spirit of the cave by cutting the animal's throat at the entrance;" a native explains the object of this by saying that "the people think there are evil spirits in some of the caves." Again, "when a newly married couple take up their residence in an old house, or any-one makes his home in a new one, it is customary to

[1] *Cp.* Briggs *in loc.*, and Kittel's *Biblia Hebraica* (notes on the text of this verse).

[2] Page 53.

take a goat or sheep upon the flat roof, and cut its throat so that the blood runs down over the lintel."[1] In connexion with this one may compare the following Midrashic comment on this verse; "Rabbi Jochanan said, 'Before a dwelling is reared up,[2] the evil spirits gather round a man, but after the habitation has been set up, no plague comes nigh thy tent.' Rabbi Simeon ben Lakish said, 'Why do we learn this out of the Psalms, for it says, The Eternal will bless thee and keep thee (Num. vi. 24)? It is because of the evil spirits.'"[3]

Taking these extracts together with the context of this verse, it is difficult to get away from the conviction that the reference is to demons; and this conviction grows stronger on considering the next verse.

Verse 11. *For His angels He will command for thee, to guard thee in all thy ways.*

If we have been correct in holding that there is little or nothing in this Psalm to show that the evil from which protection is promised is from the works of evil-disposed men, if, that is to say, this Psalm refers throughout to spiritual enemies, then this verse gains greatly in significance. Both in biblical and post-biblical Jewish theology it is taught that evil spirits work antagonistically to God and men, and that these evil spirits are fallen angels (cp. *e.g.* Isa. xiv. 12 ff.), or the offspring of fallen angels, who are finally sub-

[1] *Op. cit.* p. 184.
[2] The reference is, of course, to a tent.
[3] *Midrash Tehillim, in loc.*

jugated by the powers of heaven.[1] An echo of this warfare between the angels of God and the powers of darkness is preserved in Jude 6, and possibly a reference to the same thing underlies the strange passage vv. 12-16, in this epistle. "It is said that angels accompany the dead on their departure from this world," and that three bands of angels of the divine ministry accompany the righteous, the first singing, "He shall enter in peace," the second "They shall rest on their couches" and the third, "The one who walketh in uprighteousness " (Isa. lvii. 2); but when a wicked man departs, three bands of angels of destruction are described as accompanying him, saying, "There is no peace, saith my God, to the wicked" (Isa. lvii. 21).[2]

The thought of the verse before us is strikingly illustrated in the book of Tobit, where we read of Tobias being accompanied during his journeyings by an angel, who teaches him how to drive away an evil spirit; see especially vi. 1-7, 15-17. It is also worth recalling that this verse is quoted in the Gospels in the passage describing our Lord's temptation by the Devil (Matt. iv. 6, Luke iv. 10, 11).

Verse 12. *Upon their palms they shall bear thee, lest thou strike thy feet against a stone.*

The fact that the word *kaph*, the "palm" of the hand, is used instead of the ordinary word for hand, suggests the idea that the angels hold their hands

[1] See *e.g.*, the "Book of Enoch" (ed. Charles) *passim*, but more especially chaps. vi-xv.

[2] *Jewish Encycl.* i. 593, where many references are given.

for the man to stand upon, and in this way he is raised up wherever an obstacle lies in his path. But the placing of such obstacles would have been believed to be the work of evil spirits; and probably the idea was that they were placed in such a way as to escape notice until the harm was done; otherwise it is difficult to see why angels should be needed to prevent a man from stumbling, even if the words were used symbolically, which however, was probably not the case

Verse 13. *Upon reptile and cobra shalt thou tread; thou shalt trample (upon) the young lion and dragon.*

The Hebrew text in the first part of this verse "by a copyist's error of a single letter, introduces prematurely the lion."[1] The rendering given above agrees with the *Septuagint*, *cp.* also Deut. xxxii. 24. According to general ancient Semitic belief a relationship was believed to exist between certain animals and demons; thus, in ancient Arab belief, demons appeared in the form of wild beasts in the wilderness; the closest connexion of all was said to be between demons and serpents; *Gann* and *Ghul* have become synonymous with "serpent" in Arabic, this applies also to *Shaitan* (=Satan).[2] In Jewish demonology, too, it is taught that serpents are in league with demons; Satan is, of course, identical with the serpent in the garden of Eden (*cp.* the Midrashim *Sifre* 138*b* and *Bereshith Rabba* c. xxii., also the Babylonian Talmud, *Shabbath*

[1] Briggs, *in loc.*

[2] Wellhausen, *Op. cit.* pp. 152 ff; Robertson Smith, *The Religion of the Semites* (2nd ed. pp. 120 f., 133).

55*b*); according to *Baba Kamma* 16 *a* (Babylonian Talmud) the *Shedim* were originally serpents, and became what they are by a process of evolution.[1] Among the Babylonians all demons were conceived of as normally dwelling in animals; it was the way in which the Babylonians explained to themselves the problem as to where the permanent abode of demons was, seeing that they were excluded from the realm of the dead. Among such animals those were chosen by the demons which were likely to inspire sudden fear, more especially serpents, which appeared suddenly, one knew not whence, and disappeared as suddenly, one knew not whither. Among the Phœnicians the lion was regarded as the incarnation of a demon.[2] These facts are significant when read in connexion with the verse before us.

Verses 14-16. These concluding verses proclaim the blessedness (see note on p. 235) of him who puts his whole trust in God, Who alone can really help against spiritual enemies of every kind.

It may be added, in conclusion, that the interpretation of the psalm which has been here offered does obviously not affect the Christian use of it, excepting in a direction which must be welcome. For the thought that it is *spiritual* enemies to which the psalm refers throughout must still further endear the familiar words, and make the whole psalm more precious to us than ever.

[1] F. Weber, *Op. cit.*, pp. 252 ff.

[2] Pietschmann, *Geschichte der Phönizier*, p. 193.

INDEX OF SUBJECTS.

INDEX OF SUBJECTS.

Index of Subjects.

Index of Subjects.

Index of Subjects.

S

Q

R

Index of Subjects.

Index of Subjects.